BECOMING SUPERHUMAN:

UNLIMITED MEMORY. ULTIMATE SPEED READING TECHNIQUES. WRITE SMARTER & FASTER. ACCELERATE YOUR LEARNING, ACCELERATE YOUR LIFE.

BEN SMITH

Table of Contents

Introduction

Congratulations on purchasing *Becoming Superhuman* and thank you for doing so. This book is based on some of the methods that I used to jumpstart my freelance writing career after college. I knew that time was my most valuable resource, so I learned to make the most out of it. I named the title of this book *Becoming Superhuman because* that is what I sought to become. I didn't want to be stuck working at some 9 to 5 that I hated just to make ends meet. I didn't want to sit passively and waste my best days rotting away on the internet. Instead, I made a promise to myself to stop procrastinating and to start producing. I needed a few things to help me, like a sharper memory and better reading and writing skills. So, I wrote a book sharing the things I learned on my journey to becoming superhuman.

The book is broken into three parts. Part 1 will discuss memory techniques for accelerated learning, as well as tools for "learning how to learn" and increasing your concentration. Part 2 is all about speed reading, how to do it and why. Part 3 is about increasing your writing speed.

I hope you can learn something from me and begin your own

—

journey to become superhuman. I have learned so much after adopting the skills talked about in this book, and I've learned how to overcome writer's block in my day job. The topics covered are a little rushed, but I figured it would be better and provide more value than writing three separate books.

Thanks again for choosing this book! Every effort was made to ensure it is full of as much useful information as possible.

Please enjoy!

Part 1:
Developing Memory Skills
for Accelerated Learning

Chapter 1: The Science of Memory and the Brain

If you are wondering what the exact mechanisms of memory are in the human brain, this chapter will largely disappoint you, because these things are part of active research. What we do know is that memory is a complicated process that is difficult to pinpoint. Unlike other faculties of the mind, we can't just say that this part of the brain is responsible for remembering things, and this other part of the brain is for retrieving information. Certain phenomena such as emotion, motor control and tactile awareness each have physical locations on the brain that facilitate each function but not memory. Mapping these areas to functions is easy. You can imagine having a study were participants are hooked up to a machine that shows what part of the brain gets lit up during certain activities. Alternatively, if you are a little more imaginative, you can think of a grisly experiment were the examiner lobs off pieces of the brain and tests what functions the subject loses. Don't worry — modern experiments of this nature are more ethical now. We also know that patients suffering from brain injuries or cerebral tumors will often lose functions such as language and speech depending on what areas are afflicted.

Memory seems to be missing from these types of experiments. Before, it was thought that a person was capable of storing memories in a single brain cell or neuron. The so-called "grandmother cell" would later be experimentally verified. If a person thinks of their grandmother, then a single neuron fires. Likewise, if that person sees their grandma in real life or in a picture, the neuron fires again. This is the gnostic or reductionist theory of the mind, which has numerous problems and has been contested by most of the neuroscience community. The problem with the grandmother cell is that for it to be true, then every arbitrary piece of information we store in the brain would need a corresponding neuron. Moreover, while there are some 100 billion neurons in the average human brain, this number isn't enough for storing everything we know. The grandmother cell involves multiple processes that happen all at once. First, the brain registers the mental picture and then ascribes meaning to it. Language is a big proponent as well. When it comes to a mental representation of a word, the brain needs to fire up the language related faculties to parse what is being said and then create a link to the concept being represented. This is a signified signifier relationship where the word acts as the symbol or signifier and the concept is the signified. In other words, it is unlikely that a single neuron is responsible for the complex interaction between mental abilities that allow one to think about their grandmother.

However, if the grandmother cell and various other "gnostic" cells have been discovered experimentally, what causes them? This is an area of high contention in neuroscience, and there are no clear answers. Some believe that gnostic cells are a key insight into how memory works, while others think that they are "bugs" in our brain software. That grandmother cells have been proved to exist means that somebody has to be wrong and the other right. The main contender to the reductionist theory is the distributed or neural network theory. It could be that grandmother cells are byproducts of the mass sending of signals from neurons to neurons that for whatever reason manifest in a single one. Just because grandmother cells act as if they are the sole mechanism of certain memories, it doesn't mean that they can't be caused by something else.

This begs the question of what exactly memory is. Take a simple concept, such as riding a bike for example. Is the ability to ride one considered a sort of memory, or is it more like a combination of things? We talk about things like muscle memory, but which one is which? Certainly, the ability to ride a bike needs to be learned first, and that process of learning may be considered a type of working memory, but it still feels different from the memories we cherish, or the memories we use to remember dates and figures. I think it is safe to say that riding a bike serves as a functional type of memory that can be evoked automatically when one wishes to go somewhere via bicycle. Remembering about your first kiss is similar, but at the same time completely different. Likewise, remembering the digits of pi or the order of cards in a deck feels distinct both from the bike and kiss example. Remembering to ride a bike generally endures for a long time. If you learn how to use it once, and regularly ride one, you will probably remember how to keep riding bikes for the rest of your life.

These examples outline the basics of the different types of memory:

Long-Term Memory

- Associated with the brain's ability to remember things throughout someone's lifespan
- Long-term memory is likely created by vast interactions of neurons across brain regions
- These types of memories tend to change or mutate over time as the person synthesizes information from different sources and puts them into the memory

Implicit Memory

- The type of memory associated with doing things automatically i.e. riding a bike or driving a car
- Is a form of long-term memory
- Procedural memories fall under this category and are used to remember the order to do things like baking a cake or solving a multistep algebra problem

Declarative or Explicit Memory

- Is a type of long-term memory
- Memory that is consciously committed into the brain. For example, thinking about last night's dinner party and recalling what your crush was wearing
- Declarative memories are interesting because using conscious thought you could remember things that previously you were not explicitly aware of. It is as if the brain records everything, but you can only remember things that you consciously put a spotlight on, which leads on to the next point
- Episodic memory or autobiographical memory are memories elicited by certain events, usually those that have a strong emotional response (traumas, extreme joys, depressive events)
- Some people are said to possess a photographic memory where precise figures and events can be thought of with little exposure to them. More prevalent

in children than adults, and mostly non-existent in adults. It is hard to differentiate between what is fact and what is fiction when it comes to gauging how good claimed photographic memory is.

- Semantic memory denotes an ability to remember facts and figures from textual information. Think about someone who is "book smart"

Short-Term Memory

- Also called "working memory"
- Denotes the immediate availability of information as soon as the brain starts processing it
- When first meeting somebody new, their name is put into working memory but is often lost if this person didn't leave a lasting impression
- When information is committed to working memory the brain makes a decision whether or not it should be committed to long-term memory. This can happen consciously or unconsciously
- Short-term memory is thought to correlate directly with age and substance abuse. Getting older, smoking marijuana and drinking in excess are just a few factors that have been experimentally shown to lower short-term memory. More recently, cell phones and internet addiction have been to blame for short-term memory loss.

The various different types of memory that exist only complicate theories of human memory. According to the distributed theory of memory, the memory creating process follows a streamlined set of stages. First is the stimulus or encounter stage when the information is first noticed by the brain. This can happen in any distinct region (words and communication in the language region, faces in the visual cortex, hearing, etc.). From there, a process called "encoding" takes place that essentially remembers the neuron response from the initial stimulus. It is likely that encoding takes place in the same area of the stimulus, but could be delegated to other parts of the brain as well. The final step called "recall" or "retrieval" occurs when the same encoded signals are recreated, thus creating some semblance of the original. The distributed theory of memory also explains why even when the original regions of the brain that created the stimulus are damaged memories can still survive: the brain is a fault tolerant distributive system that can store information redundantly. Just as the internet was created for surviving targeted nuclear attacks, the brain has a design with no single failure points. This is, of course, a simplified view of what actually occurs, but a simplified view is sufficient, seeing as the brain is perhaps the most complex thing we know about.

Encoding

The way memories are encoded in neurons is perhaps one of the most mysterious aspects of remembering things. For us, the act of remembering something feels completely natural, but to the brain, it is something entirely different. Memory encoding, along with the distributed theory, speaks volumes about the complexity of the brain. Encoding occurs directly after an information stimulus takes place, and this can be anything from hearing a noise, smelling something or reading a sentence in a book. From here the encoding goes directly to the working memory for easy recall and it is either discarded or put into long-term memory.

The encoding process is strengthened by association, also called associative memory. In essence, the better your brain can associate new information with information it already knows, the easier new information is to retain. You can imagine a massive neural network made up of billions of individual neurons, each connected to imaginary concepts. The more neurons are connected to a concept, the stronger it exists in the mind. Synthesizing new information then becomes a game of how powerful the connection is, how many neurons are actively working for that concept to be represented. As you will later learn, this can be hacked for your benefit using mnemonics. A mnemonic is a simple auditory, visual or verbal association technique that creates an artificial association of concepts where previous knowledge may not have existed. Retention of information is further strengthened when these concepts are important to the person, or when they can be synchronized across domains, sometimes called "memory consolidation"

Storage

According to the distributed theory of the brain, memories are encoded, and then stored throughout the brain in the form of neural networks. Each neuron on the network may store one part of the encoded memory, and together they make up the full memory. These combinations of neurons lie dormant until the memory is procured, whether it is in working memory or long-term memory storage. When they are finally recalled by the brain, they all fire according to the encoding. This is all good and well, but the actual hardware of the storage process is less understood. We don't know, for example, how much information we can conceivably store, or for how long. Some believe that the brain is able to store arbitrary amounts of information, indefinitely. I think that such sentiments are understandable coming from the distributed theory, but they aren't very helpful. When memory is greater understood, I expect there to be good metrics on the number of pathways the brain can expect to have, and how often they are rewritten or forgotten.

Even a common-sense approach dispels the notion that the brain has infinite capabilities. The old saying "use it or lose it" rings true in this sense. Sure, you learned to use a bike when you were five, but what if you were never to use a bike again since then? Presumably, the same neural pathways that stored the procedural memories associated with riding a bike slowly fade. Maybe the brain notices that the encoding pattern hasn't fired in a while, and decides to free up computing power, just as one might free up space on their phones. This is what embarrassingly happened to me in my mid-twenties when I discovered (to my friends' horror and amusement) that I had somehow forgotten how to balance on a bike. This is why it is important to pay attention to the things you remember, and how often you use them. When I graduated from college with a measly liberal arts degree, I took it upon myself to relearn high school mathematics. I was surprised at how much of the material I had completely forgotten. Slowly I had to make my way up from elementary algebra to more complex equations.

Recall

In a way, recall or remembering things is simply the replaying of encoded memories. There are some more signals mixed in with the initial encoding. Otherwise, it would be impossible to differentiate between what is happening now and what happened before. Memory is effectively a combination of your current environment and the encoded information of the past in the form of neuronal firing. Recalling memories is split into two kinds, those of recognition and those of pure recall. You recognize something when given similar physical stimulus as when you did on the first encounter. If you are good at remembering faces, you are using your facial-recognition ability to remember them. This relies on the person or face being in front of you, though. Pure recall doesn't require any physical representation. It is when you are able to remember things from the past by simple virtue of you having experienced them at some point. Memory techniques help reinforce your pure recall ability.

Chapter 2: Harnessing Your Concentration

The first step to becoming superhuman is to achieve an adequate concentration control. What I mean by this is the ability to work on something and give it your 100%. Today's high speed, always on culture makes it difficult to attain this level of focus. I would wager that most professionals today suffer from at least some sort of distraction in the workplace. It is far too easy to open a browser and check Facebook, Twitter and YouTube accounts that do not necessarily relate to work. Some of us are hopelessly addicted to browsing these sites or playing video games in between work assignments. Don't even get me started on phones. Unless I am expecting a call, I leave it on silent if I am trying to get in the zone. As a rule of thumb, I leave my phone in another room until I have done my work.

I've found that those work from home or do freelance work are especially prone to this effect. Assignment due in 10 days? I'll put on a movie and get started on it later. This attitude can be fatal to the longevity of any self-employed work. This is true whether you are a novelist, technical writer, copywriter, programmer, heck anything that needs to be done in front of the computer really. If you are just starting out, then you are in luck. This book will teach you some ways to harness your concentration that will benefit you for the rest of your career. If you already have a concentration mindset — you are amazing. You are on your first step to becoming superhuman already. Others need to develop the attitude, as well as the skills associated with concentration. Much of what I will write is aimed towards those who work from home and are more prone to distractions, but the ideas here can be applied in the office as well.

Delaying Gratification

At the heart of the concentration mindset is understanding the power of delayed gratification. If you abnegate yourself from reward now and do the work, the rewards will double in time. Before I developed the concentration mindset, I could sit in front of my computer, literally all day and get nothing done. I don't mind just six or eight hours either. I found myself stuck in a perpetual cycle of going from one source of entertainment to the other. I would start my day, hop on my desk chair and check my social media accounts. Then I would play whatever the latest game I was addicted to was. Maybe get some food and watch it in front of the TV or put on YouTube. Then I would go on sites like Reddit, 4chan, and 9gag. I'd make the rounds going through my favorite news aggregator site just to read articles for the hell of it. Take a break, and maybe throw on another video game and do my "daily" virtual tasks. Also porn — so much porn. And what was the result of such depravity? At the end of the day would feel like a useless piece of crap that was headed nowhere and fast. One day I said that enough was enough and I slowly started building my concentration mindset.

I equate my experience with doing nothing all day to being "doped on dopamine". I was addicted to video games, true, but I was also mindlessly reading articles, checking social media and watching videos. What do these things have in common? They all stem from the same addiction, and that is the neurotransmitter dopamine. Dopamine, sometimes called the "happiness chemical" along with serotonin, takes a hitch whenever we do some pleasurable activity. Every time you scroll your feed looking at memes, reading news, or checking your phone for that elusive notification from your crush, you are effectively micro dosing on dopamine hits. And some people do this all throughout the day. I noticed this early on my journey to develop my concentration mindset when I noticed myself crawling back to these distractions. Even when I started taking up freelance writing jobs online, I would inevitably return to my video games, my Reddit and my YouTube. I would "reward" myself every several hundred words and play a quick match of Fortnite or read an article. One match turned to another, and then a few more, and before I knew it, an hour had gone by. Imagine the time sink this presented when my breaks planned for 10 minutes turned into hours.

I thought hard about this issue and I concluded that I stick by even today: frequent micro-dosing with dopamine messes with your mind. The more you get a taste for it, the more you will crave it and it starts a vicious cycle. The best way to get out of that cycle is to simply not initiate it. I ended up eliminating social media and other distractions during working days. Alternatively, if I did allow them, only at the end of the day when work for that day was finished. Who would have known that the words of my mother would bring clarity to me as an adult? "Do your homework first, play your video games later."

Trust me, the video games or YouTube videos will feel much better with the knowledge that you made money that day or the knowledge that you chipped away a few chapters on your latest novel.

Sharpen the Blade

Mastering how to delay gratification takes some time and is only a piece of the puzzle. Next comes the much-dreaded "multi-tasking" phenomena that are the bane of knowledge workers right next to procrastination. No matter how you look at it, working on one thing at a time is more productive than constantly switching from different tasks. Constant task switching combined with dopamine hits in between is a deadly combination, one that I struggled for with for the longest time. See, when I would switch from playing a video game to going on YouTube I was doing so on autopilot. I didn't know where the next dopamine hit would come from, I just knew it was coming. Sometimes I would play video games while watching YouTube without any lapse in in-game performance. But just because it works for entertainment it doesn't mean it works for productivity.

Think of your concentration as a dull blade and your work as some material your blade needs to cut through. For the most efficient cut, you want the sharpest blade. Like, single-molecule-blade sharp. It sounds counterintuitive, but the more things you work on at the same time the higher the average time for completion is. This is a little lesson I took from my time studying lean project management and lean manufacturing techniques. Under the Kanban system, there is a central philosophy and that is to "limit the work in progress." In an assembly line setting, the work in progress comprises of all the different stages and processes that material goes through. If you imagine a car plant with a single person responsible for each stage, the work in progress gets stretched out. Sure, everything is getting done at the same time, but at what cost? Assembling a car would take forever to make! Instead, if some of those stages gained a few additional workers, and the other stages were put on pause, the work at a time gets done faster.

The same principle can be applied to your work. In between reading and writing emails (or anticipating emails), doing research, checking work chat channels, and doing actual work the work in progress is all over the place. What's more, task switching suffers from "cold starts", a term I borrowed from the cloud computing world. Basically, a server takes a little while to initialize so that it can begin serving webpages. The traditional computing model is to have a server run 24/7 so that users get immediate responses, but a modern approach in cloud computing called "serverless" shuts the server down and only starts it when there is a request. Since the server doesn't run 24/7 you save on the electric bill. But since servers take a while to start up, your first response back to the user will take a little longer. Each time you task switch your mind takes some time to reacclimatize to whatever it was you were working on. Computer programming is notorious for this. It may take a programmer up to 20 minutes to get back into the "zone" after being interrupted just once. I will admit that some tasks do have a lower cold start time, but for me, the cold start for writing is particularly high.

Chapter 3: Setting the Stage for Learning: Environment and Lifestyle

The memory techniques you will learn in the coming chapters will only take you so far if you find yourself in the wrong environment. Likewise, delaying gratification will only take your concentration mindset so far if your house is full of distractions. There are certainly environments out there that are more conducive to learning and success in general. I cringe whenever I hear some politician or person from privilege accuse the misfortunate of just being lazy. I know this isn't a place for politics, but I will use this example to drive my point home. Poor students who grow up in the inner city have so many distractions they have to sort through. If you live in a housing complex with thin walls, you are dealing with constant noise. Say you are such a student and also have younger siblings you have to look after when you get home from school. Between the noise, parental responsibilities and everything else, how are you supposed to get any studying done? Add to that the constant barrage of distractions from technology and you have an uphill climb, simply because you are in the wrong place at the wrong time in your life.

I also don't believe that changing one's environment is impossible. I too suffered from a noisy house with lots of distractions around, but I was able to overcome them one by one. The easiest way is to get all your work done away from the said environment. Coffee shops and public libraries were like my home away from home when I wanted to get things done.

Noise

Unwanted ambient noise can come from many sources. The most likely culprits are pets, neighbors, busy streets, and the dreaded noisy roommate. If you find yourself surrounded by noise during studying time, you will have to do something about it. You can try buying earplugs, or a good pair of headphones. High-end noise-canceling headphones tend to work best in my experience. Noise-isolating headphones muffle ambient sounds, which is usually dependent on how snugly fit the headgear is. On the other hand, noise-canceling headphones emit frequencies into the air that nullify sounds coming in. They tend to be more comfortable, and that is why

I prefer them. You could always change your environment by getting up and going to the library, but this might be problematic for some. In whatever case, you can't go wrong investing in a good pair of noise-canceling headphones. They will augment your concentration without having to work at it (unless you count the few-hundred-dollar investments as work)

Temperature

Like noise, the temperature is an environmental factor that you seldom notice until it is causing a problem. It also relates to the inner-city kid example I gave at the beginning of the chapter. Lower income families can't always afford to put a premium on temperature control. Cold winters without central heating result in brittle bones, hands too cold to even hold a book. Hot summers result in stifling heat. Personally, I would rather brave living in the desert with no AC than living in a northern climate without heat.

I find that a colder environment (but not too cold) is optimal for studying. Somewhere between 65 and 70 degrees is the sweet spot, but that's just me.

Dopamine Distractions

There is a quote by Oscar Wilde that one of my friends in high school used to say to justify her poor decisions. "The only way to get rid of temptation is to yield to it" was the quote. She only learned it after we had a unit on Wilde during our senior year, and continued to say it well into her adult life as justification for her actions. Personally, I don't know how the English curriculum got away with teaching impressionable teenagers all about temptations and "yielding" to them. I hate this quote because it creates a false dilemma that there are only two options available to someone who is dealing with temptation. Either deal with the symptoms of withdrawal from it or go all in and do what you have to do. I believe there is at least one other option that doesn't involve either of the two. Why not set up conditions to make the temptation impossible to be fulfilled? Given enough time the temptation fades, and you certainly don't have to yield to it.

In the digital sphere, this equates to turning off your phone or putting it on airplane mode. At the very least do this during your working day and during the time you dedicate to self-learning. Doing this isn't enough though. You have to actively restrict your access to the phone. Put it on top of your fridge, in your pocket, or ask someone to hold on to it until you are done. Next disconnect from the internet on your computer. It is unfortunate that the lives of knowledge workers revolve around the computer and the computer is readily available to dole out dopamine hits. If you need to use the internet though, you have to be extremely careful not to get sidetracked. A single link can turn into five and pretty soon you are down the rabbit hole of procrastination. One of the things that I do is to run a new window in private browsing mode so that my social media sessions are destroyed. Being in private browsing alone tells my brain that I'm entering working mode and not to bother looking up time-wasting activities.

Take breaks as necessary, especially if you are using the Pomodoro technique that you will learn in Chapter 5 but don't reward yourself by going back on social media. One, this will tailor your mind into thinking that you are only working for that sweet dopamine release when you go on break. Two, you might end up staying longer than you had intended. And three, rewarding yourself consistently doesn't allow your brain to de-load from the cognitive tasks you are undertaking and the extra dopamine rush. I've tried rewarding myself with short bursts of video games before. If my break was scheduled for 30 minutes, I figure that's enough time for a game of

Fortnite. The problem is that as you can guess, sometimes I would die early and I would keep playing because that game "didn't count". If you repeat this enough times, you have a serious issue hiding in plain sight. Those measly 30 minutes never had a chance.

Healthy alternatives during the break involve doing light exercise like getting up from your seat and walking around. If your workplace has a large campus, go outside and get some fresh air. Why not? Prolonged sitting is bad for you anyways. If there are people around, and if your break time permits it, start a little conversation with someone. Talk to them about how your work or study day is going. Share ideas with each other. I think this was the original purpose of putting water coolers in remote areas in the workplace: to give employees an excuse to get up and to practice their social skills. Whatever it is you do, it should be gentle on the old brain waves. Abstain from answering stressful emails, but feel free to answer those low priority ones. Clean out your inbox if it can be helped. Avoid starting or working on similar intellectual pursuits if your breaks are shorter than 30 minutes. As a general rule, I won't do the same kind of work during break that I was doing previously. If I am working on a novel, I won't start writing a new one. Conversely, If I am doing technical documentation, I won't open a word document for a short story I've been working on. Sometimes I'll do math problems in my head to exercise my memory and arithmetic skills at the same time. Another great option is doing a few rounds on Duolingo to learn a new language. It's free, fun and rewarding!

Lifestyle-Specific Factors

You've made the decision to become superhuman—congratulations! But you have to take care of 3 dogs, 1 cat, 2 toddlers, and a hungry spouse—not ideal conditions for learning. If you are a self-learner or freelancer, make sure you sort the house economy before you do anything else. You don't need to reserve 8 hours a day to become a superhuman (though dedicating more time certainly helps). Four or even two hours a day is more than enough to begin increasing your memory and getting things done. That being said, the lifestyle choices you make outside of your studies will affect how you ultimately learn. If you aren't getting an adequate diet your mental performance may suffer. Studies have shown the benefits that good exercise has on the mind. The same can be said for sleep. If you aren't getting at least 7-8 hours a night, you are doing it wrong. The image of the superhuman isn't some college kid up at 3 am pounding down red bulls and

—

Oreos for sustenance. At least that's not my picture of a superhuman. For me, being superhuman is the definition of self-discipline. It means going to bed at a good hour and waking in the morning. Instead of staying in bed for thirty minutes up to an hour browsing social media, this person is out lifting weights or jogging down the street.

Cramming information last minute might work for passing exams but 80% of that information begins to fade away mere weeks after the exam was taken. College grads only retain a small percentage of the overall knowledge that they learn during their undergraduate problems. Why? Because the vast majority of them only learn information to later regurgitate it during midterm exams and term papers. They learn for the sake of getting a grade, not for the sake of gaining knowledge. If you are one of those people who never went to college or left early but still want to have the student mindset, don't sweat it. I can tell you in full confidence that you don't need a college education to learn things anymore. If anything, the degree might actually give you bad learning habits based on rote memorization rather than the cross-domain consolidation of knowledge.

Chapter 4: Memory Techniques

Enhancing your memory skills goes hand in hand with accelerated learning and becoming superhuman. If you remember how memory works, information is first digested and held in working memory before the brain consolidates it into long-term memory. The more neural connections you can make to other concepts, the better. This is why learning something new strengthens memory, and strengthening memory allows you to learn better and easier. The greater the expanse of your personal knowledge that you keep in your head the more resources that are at your disposal to make meaningful connections between diverse fields. When I was in college working at my liberal arts degree, I took classes in philosophy, science, math and computer science. While I didn't learn in-depth knowledge in any of these fields as an undergrad, I did learn a solid foundation in all of them. This initial seed of knowledge led me on a journey to devour more and more books. I wanted to learn as much as I could about all of these topics. Before I knew it, I was making connections between the mathematical foundations of computer science and applying philosophy to concepts like artificial intelligence.

But before you get to long-term connection making, memory techniques help create an artificial connectiveness in the brain. You can remember almost anything you want to without having any background knowledge on the topic you are studying. These memory techniques can also help you in your daily life. When I started driving, I vowed never to use a cell phone or GPS device when I was going places. I was able to memorize the major streets of my home city well. Memory techniques helped me do that. I don't even need to make shopping lists anymore because I can memorize up to fifty items without even thinking about it twice. Okay, maybe not that easily. There is some mental preparation that goes into solidifying memory when you use these techniques. The more you do them, the more automatic they become, but it definitely requires effort on your part.

I want to dispel the myth that memory comes naturally. It really doesn't. More precisely, memory is an art that must be perfected. The Greeks and Romans practiced it like any other liberal art during the time. If you wanted to be a great orator, you better have had an amazing memory. Socrates was famously against writing systems because he thought his students would get lazy. Why bother exercising your memory muscles when a pupil could simply write things down? Of course, back then writing wasn't a fundamental skill like it is now. Things have changed, and the art of memory has fallen into obscurity. It's a pity that it has because learning how to memorize things unlocks a plethora of benefits for students and knowledge workers alike. Now if someone needs to look up a figure, they just ask good old Dr. Google. Modern-day teachers complain that their millennial and generation Z students are too reliant on technology. As a millennial, I can attest to that fact.

I remember asking a younger cousin not too long ago if he knew how to get to the closest Wal-Mart from his house (he was learning how to drive at the time). He said that he could, but he would have to look it up first on his phone. Just ask any young person today for directions or historical figures and watch them fumble for their devices. It seems that phones have replaced writing systems when it comes to threatening our memory capabilities. Perhaps Socrates did have a point after all. Maybe his sagely wisdom allowed him to see a future were the citizens of Athens would have to rely on external implements to recall important information. I fear that today there are too many people who can't even tell you their own phone numbers without looking at their contact list, let alone the number of their parents or close friends.

Memory by Association

Here is a quick exercise to test your current working memory. On the left is a list of fruits you may recognize, while on the right there is a random list of things and concepts. Chances are that you are more likely to memorize the fruits because they are familiar, and logically belong to the same set. Your mind is more readily available to memorize them because they are alike. How many fruits can you even name off the top of your head? Chances you will think of most of the fruits on the left side. By contrast, there is no easy way to group or associate the terms on the right. This is where memory becomes a trained skill rather than an automatic faculty of the mind.

Get a timer out and set it for 2 minutes. Commit to memory every item on the lists below during that span of time. When the timer is finished start another timer for 1 minute and thirty seconds, try to write down as many as you can.

Fruits – Strong Association

1. Strawberry
2. Apple
3. Banana
4. Kiwi
5. Orange

Random things – weak association

1. Stapler
2. October
3. Algebra
4. Toyota

6. Blueberry	5. Function
7. Mango	6. Napkin
8. Papaya	7. Couch
9. Pear	8. Bulldozer
10. Pomegranate	9. Ocelot
	10. Neptune

How did you do? If you were able to write down at least 8 on each list—fantastic! You already have an excellent working memory. It's okay if you didn't get as much on the weak association side, that is to be expected. Likewise, if you didn't do so well in the first list that's okay. It probably means that you were trying to remember from memory rather than from association. If you know that apple was a fruit on the list, you should be able to remember that oranges are on there too because both are common fruits. Raw memory ability does help quite a bit here. Even without making associations for the second list, it is possible to memorize these quite easily.

So how would you form associations from a random garbled list of words? My favorite way of doing this is by creating a short story in your head that involves each term. For whatever reason, humans are tuned for remembering stories. I think it has something to do with episodic memory and probably aided in survival as well. If someone from your tribe says not to go to the craggy rocks because he saw lions in there, you will immediately commit it to memory. Your stories don't have to be so adrenaline-inducing, however. Here is a simple one you could have used to memorize the right column. It doesn't even have to make sense so long you tell a story.

1. The grading quarter ends in **October** time to get the **Staple**r out.
2. Students learned **Algebra functions** and the planet **Neptune**
3. I left my bagel and **napkin** on the **couch.**
4. I should get them before **Bulldozer** my pet **Ocelot** finds them.
5. Then I'll have to throw him in the back of the **Toyota**

The beauty of this technique is that you can even gleam temporal order from the events in the story. Association is one thing, remembering order is another. The order doesn't always matter, but sometimes it does (remembering the digits of pi, for example). Procedural or historic knowledge also require things to be remembered in sequence. Here's an example story for the fruit list with order preserved. Notice that it is more difficult to map a story with terms that are already strongly associated.

1. **Strawberry** shortcake went to town.
2. The market had **Apples** and **Bananas** on display
3. She took a **Kiwi** purse and a big **Orange** hat

4. Her **Blue Berry** eyes lit up when she saw the fresh **Mangos**

5. A vendor made her a P smoothie – **Papaya, Pear, and Pomegranate**

Practice writing the lists in order now using the storytelling technique. Not only will you be able to remember the individual terms, but their order as well.

Here is a random list of words, see how much you can memorize on your own using the story technique. Double points for remembering in order. It doesn't matter how long it takes to memorize them so long as you are able to reproduce the list. If you don't like the order, feel free to come up with your own. After you can memorize this arbitrary list of words, see if you can compile your own list and do the same with them.

Knife	Washington	Topology	Nuclear
Table	Parrot	Red	Entity
Stars	Inheritance	Fall	Hair
Minotaur	Abacus	Run	Claw

I will admit that this is a simplified view into memory by association, but you can already begin to notice the underlying concepts. The storytelling technique is useful for remembering shopping lists, and I've used it on many a visit to the supermarket. The real trouble comes when you need to remember longer lists (say up to 50 terms) by telling a story. In that case, the challenge becomes remembering the story, which requires raw memory skills. A temporal order of events does help, but cramming in 50 terms in ways that make little sense probably isn't the best approach. I still remember taking Sunday school classes at our local church when I was little. One of the first things they had us do was memorize the Lord's Prayer, so we could recite it on each meeting. The good thing with stories is that you don't have to recite them exactly as if you were saying a prayer. If you remember the gist of the events and the order of terms, you can switch words up. The terms are really what you are after, not accuracy.

Method of Loci

Greek orators were renowned for their memory abilities. Seneca is quoted as being able to recall two-thousand names in the order they were given. In a class of some two hundred students, Seneca could also listen to each recite their poetry and then repeat it back to them in reverse order, starting from the last student to the first. Augustine was known to recite

Virgil in its entirety backward. These masters of memory could not only remember things but also tap into them with an arbitrary order. While there is little application to such feats of memory, they nevertheless illustrate what the human mind is capable of, especially in regard to the art of memory. The method of loci comes directly from the ancient Greek practice of the art of memory. A locus is a focal point — a place that you can easily visualize in the mind. This can be anywhere but is usually reserved for manmade structures like houses, buildings, street corners and so on. The Greeks referred to something called the "artificial memory" that is based on a visual mapping of information. In order to remember specifics of something, you have to create an artificial association inside your mind. Each new idea or concept has its own locus that can then easily connect to previous loci. Each locus is paired with some image or visual representation of the idea. Here the Greeks advise that the images should be noteworthy, rather than banal. The mind tends to remember things that pop out at us, whether they are exceptionally pretty or exceptionally horrific. Comedic images get the brain working better than regular images. The absurd and surreal also have a stake in memory. Things that out of the ordinary stick out, and we tend to remember them. If you can make an emotional connection, then go for it.

A locus can be almost anything, but it has to be familiar to you like the back of your hand. Additionally, the locus must lend itself to spatial awareness and spatial relationships. These are the main two properties that make the method of loci an effective memory technique: familiarity and distance relationships. This is why structures are the preferred type of loci, you know them intimately and they are spacious containers of things. Chances are, you can recall with high accuracy the layout of your childhood home and the following houses or apartments that you inhabited for the rest of your life. Why is this? The human mind is constantly interacting with the environment. Some neural imprint in your brain says this is my house, I walk in through the front door and I see the living room and kitchen area, and a hallway leading to bedrooms. What's more, you interact with places every day. It becomes automatic, long-term procedural memory like learning to ride a bike. You might forget why you went into a room at times, but you will never forget how it is you got there.

As long as the two requirements of familiarity and space are met, anything can be a locus. Your car, for example, is very familiar to you and has spatial relations between the hood, dashboard, driver and passenger seats, cup holder, trunk and so on. The workplace is another great example. I used to work at a small coffee place at the local mall that served pastries. I knew where the bread was located, the ingredients, cleaning supplies, storage area and the route I would take to get there from the mall entrance. The same can be said of my favorite buildings from the university I attended. I spent far too much time in the library and became familiar with the general layout of all four floors of it including the basement. Growing up, one of my favorite shows to watch was Two and a Half Men. I watched reruns almost every day during middle and high school. I watched it so much that I can still recall the general layout of Charlie Harper's Malibu two-story beach house. There was the front porch area, living room with bookshelf and piano, a kitchen and outdoor deck, three different rooms one with its own bathroom.

The method goes something like this. You visualize a house (or any suitable locus) and you "store" information at various points of focus or *loci.* The easiest version of this is to store information in each room. Most houses only have around four or five rooms, so you can imagine this method only allows a few points of focus. Next for each point of focus and for each piece of information you want to memorize, create an image association that will stick in your mind. The more absurd, violent, emotional, or sexual in nature the image the better it will stick.

I'm going to walk you through an arbitrary memorization exercise using the loci method. For this exercise, I want you to memorize the following sequence of words in order:

1. Kennedy
2. Sausage
3. Ribcage
4. Pfizer
5. Desert
6. Loop
7. Skin
8. Cartridge
9. Cantaloupe
10. Pan

Look at these words for a minute and then see if you can recall them in order. You probably can't, so I will show you how I typically use this method to remember things in sequence. I'll use a generic example first. Shocking images tend to work best for memorizing things, but I will leave things relatively clean. The loci for this example focus on a student housing apartment. The technique begins at the front door.

1. Instead of there being a regular peephole below the apartment number, there is a picture of John F. **Kennedy** with a small hole in place where his mouth should be. Upon further inspection, you realize that the mouth is the peephole.

2. You enter the apartment through the
   before tripping over a large welcom
   raw German bratwurst **Sausage**.

3. You are greeted by a single column
   calendar open with today's month. The pictu
   calendar is a photograph of a dusty old **Ribcage**
   human specimen.

4. To the left of the wall there is a kitchen area and to the
   right is a living room. You decide to go to the left first.
   The kitchen table is littered with newspapers on top of
   which someone has written the word "**Pfizer**" in all
   caps using a deep red ink.

5. You open the fridge to see a cake-like dessert that
   appears to be a diorama of the Sonoran **Desert.** There
   are little cacti sticking out. They look delicious.

6. Next, you head back to the wall with the calendar on it
   and walk into the living room. There is a strange
   substance floating in the air. It's a cloudy green thing
   that spirals in a **Loop** around the couches.

7. As you step on the living room floor you realize it is
   squishy and you almost jump when you look down. It's
   made from human **Skin**. The complexion is slightly tan
   or golden brown.

8. You leave the living room and encounter a hallway
   where someone has left a large ink **Cartridge** with its
   spilled contents all over the floor. Your white shoes

ecome stained with a deep black.

There is one bathroom and one bedroom. You approach the bathroom and let out a gasp. Someone has bought hideous shower curtains that are blown up photographs of split **Cantaloupes**. The seeds remind you of something gross.

10. Finally, you go into the bedroom, where there is a man sitting in front of a computer wearing a metallic **Pan** as a hat.

I want you to visualize each description as vividly as you can in your head. Then, put them all together and imagine yourself arriving at the front door and making your way to the final room. You should have very little difficulty reciting these words now. Can you recite them backward too? Sure, you can! Just start in the bedroom with the man with the pan and work your way to the front door. Notice how each individual locus easily transitions to the next word in the sequence.

Mnemonics

Mnemonics are memory techniques used to retrieve information. They use a form of encoding (auditory, visual, etc.) that directly stimulates long-term memory to make things easier to memorize. They also stem from ancient Greek practices (no surprise). If you have ever taken high school level algebra, you should already be familiar with a few of these. There's PEMDAS (please excuse my dear aunt sally) or parentheses, exponents, multiplication, division, addition, and subtraction. And everyone's favorite, FOIL (first, outer, inner, last). These acronyms belong to a type of naming mnemonic that uses the first letter of a word in a string of ideas. Another commonly used mnemonic is when dialing phone numbers. You can dial something like 1-800-PANTS and get a real phone number because most dial pads map three letters to a digit.

Exercises for Part 1

1. The method of loci example above is relatively simple. You only had to remember a single word in a sequence. What I didn't tell you is that each one of these words can serve as a keyword for information. See, remembering the keyword is only half of the method. The other half is associating the keyword with an idea or concept. If you had to memorize a speech you could do it line by line or, you could come up with keywords

---

for each paragraph and memorize those. For this exercise I want you to memorize some textual information. It can be a poem, a speech, or something you read in a book. What matters is that you successfully transfer textual information into your own imaginary house.

2. This next exercise a little more complex, but doable with practice. I want you to memorize all of the United States Presidents using the same method of loci from before. There are now 45 presidents, so you will have to stretch your imagination to come up with 45 keywords to attach to 45 areas in your imaginary house.

Chapter 5: Effective Learning Tools for Students and Lifelong Learners

I had a desire years ago to learn as much as I could about the world. This resulted in my buying tons of books and never reading them. I bookmarked article after article thinking I would one day go back to it but always failing to do so. My browser history is a graveyard of information I never touched. Part of this was due to my half-assed attempts at learning. I would allow myself four hours a day to work on learning projects, and those four hours usually ended up going to YouTube or social media. I wanted to learn, but I wasn't motivated enough. I had all the resources I could ask for at my fingertips. YouTube lectures, eBooks, Wikipedia, free online tutorials, you name it. In the end, it meant nothing—I wasn't using them, and I learned very little about the topics that interested me. To quote internet columnist and blogger Clay Shirky, the problem "is not information overload. It's filter failure". In other words, it's not that I was overwhelmed by the options available to me, but that I didn't know how to sift through those options and pick a course of study.

Over time I got fed up with the perpetual cycle of information, motivation, overload, and then laziness. I started researching ways that I could improve the learning process. Since my efforts were all self-directed, I figured I needed at least something to go off. I didn't have syllabus or deadlines to keep me moving. Instead, I had to rely on my weak self-discipline and capricious attention span. I put down my projects and put all my energy into learning how I was going to learn. I learned many lessons along the way, including ways to strengthen my self-discipline and how to effectively filter useless information. I needed some direction, so my first step was taking a Coursera course called "Learning how to learn". This is essentially an online course based on Dr. Barbara Oakley's book *A Mind for Numbers*, and it is free. I highly recommend both to my readers.

Learning How to Learn

To learn how to learn something new, whether it is a skill, art or information synthesis, you must first understand what learning is. In the first chapter, I touched on the neurobiology of the brain as it pertains to memories. The distributed theory of the brain posits that neurons (brain cells) "talk" to each other to encode information. They do this by forming synapses or connections with other neurons forming a sort of network. Imagine how a social network works. People are connected to other people by their friends and mutual friends. The most popular nodes on the network have the most connections, bridging diverse social circles together. While there are only some billion neurons in the brain, there are many more orders of magnitudes of possible synapses that information can flow through. I'm talking a million billion different connections. Remember how I said the most complex thing known to man is the human brain? Yep, that's pretty much why. The task of finding out exactly how and what information is passed through those billions of connections is staggering.

I'm going to be straight with you. Learning is hard. One of the principle reasons why we procrastinate is because the brain feels a pain response associated with those things you don't want to do. Whether it's a difficult conversation you are putting off or a research paper, the brain will prefer to do something that is more pleasurable. The more you dread doing something the more it eats away at your motivation. I could tell you do simply stop dreading things and start doing them, but that is a short-sighted view of motivation. Plus, it goes against basic neurobiology. The mind wants dopamine and it will do all that it can to avoid pain. The trick is to learn how to tolerate it. Building up your mental pain tolerance makes you more resilient against those urges to stop what you are doing and put on some Netflix instead.

For the less mathematically inclined, when was the last time you really struggled through a number problem? When was the last time you had to do a calculation in your head and you didn't pull out the calculator app on your phone? Chances are, it's been a while. The same principle of mental discomfort is at work here. When your mind is faced with a difficult math problem, it is working hard to find the solution. Most people would rather not work hard. I'm one of them. I had to face the same mental anguish of keeping to it. In the end, the rewards are well worth it. Your self-discipline increases, and you see the world differently. If you have goals you want to meet, this is especially true. I mean, if you truly, truly want to achieve them. I wanted to publish novels, start my own online business, become a freelance writer, create my own personal knowledge database and to live off passive income. Quite lofty goals indeed! I still want to do those things and I actively work towards them. I'm sure you have your own lofty goals. Learning how to power through the hard stuff will get you there. My high school economics teacher once told me that taking his class would change my life. It didn't, but that was only because I was too young and too dumb to understand the implications of opportunity cost. Sure, I could be playing video games all day, or I could get a part-time job that pays minimum wage. Every hour wasted on a virtual game effectively cost me minimum wage, which was around $8.75 at the time. The return on investment on learning new skills is even more than that. If it leads to new business insights or a new career, active learning is far more valuable than playing a silly game or flipping burgers.

Diffused vs. Focused Thinking

When you are actively trying to learn something, or you find yourself starting at an algebra problem trying to find the solution, your mind is in focused mode. Focused mode is when you experience the most frustration when learning new things. You get the idea that "you just won't get it" or that you aren't a "math person". But you have to keep working at it. If math doesn't come easily to you, for example, it is a sign that you have to work harder. After you create new neural connections by forcing yourself to learn in this way, the process becomes easier.

Something few college students and self-learners understand is that studying more can be bad for you. The mind can only support so much time in the focused mode before you get diminishing returns on learning the material. This is because the brain needs rest. You need to allow it to "wander" and subconsciously play with the ideas that you gained from the focused mode. This is called diffused learning and it is responsible for all those great ideas you had in the middle of a shower. Cramming simply doesn't work.

Spaced Repetition

It is under the diffuse mode of thinking that concepts are truly learned and internalized. Learning to harness the diffuse mode involves spreading out your studying over the course of a day, week or month. The second thing you must do is constantly exercise your memory to recall the concepts you learned. So, go over your notes, visit the structures you created with the method of loci, practice math, and do these things like if they were daily habits. Understand that procrastination is the mind's way of running away from a tough mental problem. If you don't train your ability to push through procrastination, you will never become superhuman. One way you can combat procrastination is by using the Pomodoro technique.

I first started using the Pomodoro technique towards the end of college. The idea is simple. You start a timer for 25 minutes during which you will do intense work. This means no distractions, no backtracking and no getting up from your seat. If you are writing, this probably means no exiting the word processor program until the time is up. It sounds onerous, but 25 minutes go by in a flash. After the timer starts beeping, set a new timer for a five-minute break. Congratulations, you finished your first Pomodoro! A good habit is to do a 3 or four Pomodoros a day. Everybody is a little different. My favorite scheme is to do at least 8 Pomodoros, each lasting 30 minutes long with a five-minute break and a 40-minute break after four.

Lastly, and I already mentioned this in Chapter 3, but make sure you are getting regular exercise and plenty of sleep. If I told you that exercising is one of the few ways to create new neurons in your brain you would probably jump on the floor and start doing pushups. Well, it's true! If I told you that sleeping is reserved for making new neural connections in the brain and synthesis information, would you still only get 5 or 6 hours a night? Doubtful. Sleeping is learning with no mental cost, why would you skip on it?

Part 2:

Learning How to Speed read

(300% improvement)

Chapter 6: Your Mind on Reading

When I decided I would try to learn as much as possible about things that interested me, reading was the primary tool to transfer that knowledge from the world into my brain. The good news is that the internet is rife with reading material, from free e-books and Wikipedia articles to sophisticated conversations on sites like Reddit. Yes, there are serious conversations that you can learn a lot from in the Reddit comment section. I realized early on that I would never be able to read every book in its entirety. I filled my hard-drive with gigabytes of pdf's I found online or torrented — all on equally diverse fields such as energy, transportation, philosophy, psychology and so on. I also compiled a long list of works of fiction that I always wanted to read but never found the time to indulge in. As a budding novelist, I was interested in reading the works of renowned writers like King, R.R. Martin, Le Guin, and Ian M. Banks just to name a few. Whenever I found the time to indulge in some of these books, I would read them slowly and deliberately, paying attention to the writer's vocabulary and rhythm.

I treated informational books and articles a little differently. Sometimes I would skim through the book, reading a few paragraphs here and there in each chapter. The more I read online material the quicker I could decide whether an article was worth reading. I could skim through one in a few minutes and decide for myself it was full of bull, or if it was irrelevant to my interests. I downloaded electronic versions of many old textbooks, some of which I read cover to cover and thoroughly marked them up with annotating software. There are still hundreds, if not thousands of books on my hard-drive that I haven't opened yet but that I still hope to one day index in my mind somehow. The upside to being an unemployed recent college grad living with their parents is that you have way too much time on your hands. I took that period in my life to expand my knowledge before deciding on what topics I would specialize in. I know that not everyone has the time to read anymore. We all lead such busy lives and whatever downtime we do get is usually reserved for relaxation or home logistics. This is why I emphasize the power of speed reading. A book that would normally take you a week to read can be finished in as little as three days. If you are unfamiliar, there are many different speed reading techniques that I will share to get you started. But first, I should talk a little bit about reading in general.

Why read books?

It goes without saying but learning and reading go hand in hand. If you are someone who doesn't read a whole lot, you are sorely missing out. I used to like to idea of reading, but could never avert my attention from the other things I was doing. I would rather watch a YouTube video than pick up a book. Even when I started downloading e-books, I preferred to do other things than actually read them. Over time I learned how to increase my attention span and got rid of time-consuming tasks that didn't contribute to my goals. I saw a refuge in reading from the onslaught of dopamine-rich digital media. At first, I couldn't read very much. I would down a few pages and go check up on my social media. Needless to say, it took a long time to finish what I was reading. I would read the first chapter, move on to other things, and never touch the book again.

When I was in college, I did a fair bit of reading for my liberal arts classes, but I had little choice because I wanted to keep good grades. I read maybe four books a year that weren't related to school work. For me, this number was abysmally low. The only time I got to read was on my way home waiting for public transportation and during the trip there. As I got older, the more I realized that this was a conscious choice I was making rather than a metric of time constraints. I could easily have read double the number if I made reading a daily habit. If, for example, I didn't have class that day, I wouldn't get on the bus to school and I wouldn't read. Simple as that. When I wasn't studying, I was probably just wasting my time online. I would make breakfast at home and sit down at the T.V or in my room and put on some YouTube as I wolfed down my eggs and bacon. I could have easily been reading instead. Physical books are great because you can take them anywhere and therefore read them anywhere too. I only discovered this towards the end of my undergrad career. Instead of going on my phone while waiting for lecture halls to empty I would pull out a book and chip away at a few pages. I took physical books other places too. When asked to hang out with friends I always took a book with me because I knew we would end up somewhere that had a line. While it sounds rude, keep in mind that my friends would often go on their phones during downtime anyways (waiting for food to be served, stuck in line, etc.). I took books with me when I had to sit on the toilet; a risky but rewarding experience.

The more I eased into opportunistic reading the more

strangely I felt. My gut instinct was that I was doing something wrong. That reading at every chance I got was unnatural. I wasn't socializing as much (on the bus, for example. But who talks to strangers on the bus?). And I was giving up personal inner monologue time in exchange for reading the inner monologue of the author. But deep down I knew that I was doing the right thing. After all, you don't become superhuman without taking some sacrifices in your life. The trick was to figure out how much of it I could tolerate it without changing my emotional state. All I knew was that college left me feeling empty and that I had to read more and read it now while I still had the time.

If nothing else, I recommend everyone read to exercise their will above the digital tide. Even if you read on an e-reader, the same principles of concentration apply. The further you can dig into a book without losing focus, the stronger your concentration muscles become.

Why read fiction?

The kinds of books that sell best in today's markets aren't action thrillers. Instead, it is the "brainy" books written by well-known authors in their respective fields in the sciences

---

and technology. These so-called "pop science" books are able to distill complex information into digestible 300 to 400-page long books. The problem with these types of books is that they provide less dense material than a textbook and are chock-full with filler like anecdotes and the author's personal experiences. These books while entertaining and intellectually satiating tend to focus on a handful of ideas throughout. Indeed, many can be summarized with one central theme. Incidentally, I find myself plowing through these books in a matter of days or even hours because of how easy the ideas are to isolate from the fluff.

Fiction, on the other hand, presents a fuller experience. Not as dense as textbooks and not as fluffed as pop science, works of fiction (especially the good ones) provide a good balance between the two. You won't learn much by way of new information, but you get to experience the lives of the characters as if they were your own. Studies conducted by neuroscientists have shown that reading compelling works of fiction activates the same brain regions associated with the emotions and traumas undergone by the main characters. Consider classic books in literature like Huxley's *Brave New World,* Austen's *Pride and Prejudice* or Kafka's *The Trial.* When I first read these books in high school, I could almost feel my mind expanding once I took in the deeper meaning behind the works. Not expanding in a purely knowledgeable sense but in a humanitarian one. I felt like a more complete person. When you read fiction, you activate a different kind of beast, one that follows the characteristics of knowledge and empathy at the same time. You feel more connected to society and the world as a whole. Your experience becomes less unique, and more just a "possible" one in a sea of different perspectives. When I was reading *The Trial,* I was in between transitioning from high school to college life. The first thing that struck me about the university I attended were the towering buildings belonging to the different school departments. It reminded me of the scene in the book where Joseph K. is summoned for trial before the towering figures of the court bureaucracy system. I had my own fair share of bureaucratic shenanigans in college, and I came to realize that the experience is almost universal when dealing with a large institution like academia. Everyone goes through it at one point in their lives. In a way we are all Joseph K.

The Case for Speed reading

When people talk about the benefits of reading, they are usually talking about the slow, deliberate practice of reading rather than speed reading. Some go on to say that speed reading is a bastardization of literacy, that it is "lazy" and has virtually no benefits in places where it has detriments. I have read both deliberately slow and deliberately fast, about 200 words per minute on the low end and up to 600 words per minute on the high end. I can tell you that there is a difference to both speeds, but one is not inherently better. If you are reading dense material, you will need to slow down to understand certain passages, period. If you are reading less dense material, you can read at the speed of light and still have a pretty good idea of what you are looking at. It all depends on your goals.

As a superhuman, my goals were to ingest as much information as possible in as little time. I did what I call the shotgun approach to reading new things where I would read five or six books at the same time, all using speed reading techniques. The trick is to power through the easy stuff, mark what you don't understand, and go back to it later. I don't think anyone who makes the case for speed reading is also saying that you will have 100 percent reading comprehension. This is because even reading at a moderate 100 to 150 words a minute pace you won't always understand what you read. Think heavy philosophy writing, for example. Those type of texts usually need supplemental material just to understand the arguments that the writers are making. As for less dense reading like popular science books, yeah, I breeze through them. I don't feel guilty doing it either because I use annotating software to mark things. If you are looking for a free annotator for Windows systems, try PDF-XChange Viewer. The lite version includes comments and a highlighter tool. When I read fiction, I usually keep it to a pace of 200 – 250 words per minute, because reading at that speed is most pleasurable to me. However, there are times when I will go as fast as 400 – 600 words per minute on select works of fiction.

Chapter 7: Beginning Speed Reading Techniques

Like any other skill, speed reading requires practice. There are methods you can follow, but ultimately it is up to you to decide what works best. Ask yourself what your goals are. I invite you to find passages from low- and high-density material, count the words out with an online tool like https://wordcounttools.com/ and time yourself reading each. For low-density reading just look up common online tabloids and articles, for high-density reading any electronic textbook or science related Wikipedia article should suffice. The average adult reading speed is billed around 150-200 words per minute. The first step to augmenting your reading speed is to know your base speed. This is the speed you'd normally use to digest media with HIGH comprehension. Nowadays, skimming is the norm. I'm not talking about skimming, though. I mean to say a speed that you would read study material that you would be tested on for comprehension, not for the purpose of satisfying information glut. I believe that anyone can reach speeds of

600 words per minute or a 300% increase of the average with enough comprehension to write accurate word summaries. Again, you won't be able to write an exact rendition of ideas, but I promise you will get the gist of it at 600 words per minute.

You may think this isn't really "reading" and maybe you are correct in that assertion. I won't argue semantics here, but I will say that processing information from page to brain can happen at astounding speeds. I do believe this has something to do with the subconscious ability to process language and ideas. As long as your eyes see the word, and your brain registers it as the correct linguistic symbol intended by the author, I believe you get some comprehension. If it works for me it will probably work for you as well. As you become proficient in speed reading you will develop what I can a "hawk's eye" that is able to lock onto specific information as you are looking for it. Normally, if you speed read through a passage you will overlook exact figures like dates, numbers, quantities etc. But if they are important to you, I guarantee you will make a note of them.

Preliminaries

The first thing I recommend people new to speed reading is to get a feel for the book. If it is an article, then you can look up the terms in the title that you aren't sure about. Otherwise, take a look at the table of contents and read the preface, if available. Read whatever other material you can find on the book jacket. When you have background knowledge of something, making associations is that much simpler. Next, ask questions about what you are about to read. It helps to write this down because juggling memory while speed reading is a form of multi-tasking and it will slow you down. The questions can be about anything as long as it relates to the information presented in the table of contents. You may find answers to these questions, you may not. Also, keep in mind questions that you have before opening the book or article. What do you hope to gain from the reading material? What other concepts or personal knowledge are you looking to make associations to?

Here is an example table of contents from Vaclav Smil's *Energy and Civilization: A History* and some of the questions I would make before reading.

1. Energy and Society

    a. What is society referring to here? Is it a particular society or groups?

    b. What groups does the author focus on?

    c. In what context is energy talked about (purely engineering focused vs more historic)?

    d. How has energy affected society in the way that the author presents it?

    e. What benefits does society gain from energy?

    f. What is energy?

    g. How is energy represented?

2. Energy in Prehistory

    a. What groups is the author talking about here?

    b. What date ranges does "prehistory" entail

    c. Approximately what were the energy outputs for this time period?

3. Traditional Farming

    a. When did traditional farming begin?

    b. What social and economic changes caused farming to arise?

    c. How did life improve after the introduction of farming?

    d. How did life get worse after the introduction of farming?

4. Preindustrial Prime Movers and Fuels

    a. What is a prime mover?

    b. What was the best prime mover at the time?

c. What is the distinction between preindustrial and industrial society?

5. Fossil Fuels, Primary Electricity and Renewables
   a. When was electricity first discovered?
   b. What is a renewable?
   c. What does the author think about the mass usage of fossil fuels today?
   d. Does the author broach the climate change debate?

6. Fossil-Fueled Society
   a. What does the author have to say about the transformation of society?
   b. Does the author talk about demographics and fossil-fuel use in emerging economies?

7. Energy in World History
   a. What connections does the author make between the role of energy and the way history played out?
   b. Where is energy currently headed on the long view of history?

Keep these questions in mind as you read, and create new questions based on the information that you learn. Feel free to write them down again, or just keep a few in working memory as you go.

Meta-Guiding

As you can probably guess, it helps to guide your eyes with some sort of device (finger, ruler, pencil, etc.) across the page as you read. There a few ways you can do this, so feel free to experiment with different movements.

Move-as-you-go Reading

This is probably the most basic technique yet the most versatile. It is the one I use most of the time. Using a pointer (finger, pen, pencil, mouse cursor) you follow the words of the text as if you were reading them. The starting position is the left margin, and you gradually move the pointer across the page towards the right margin until you finish the line and then bring the pointer back to the left margin back you go down one line. You want to use the pointer as a rough guideline, not an exact one. Your eyes should be in front of the cursor at all times, meaning that if your pointer is on a word, you should have already processed it in your mind.

This is a versatile method because you can easily increase

your speed by reading more than one word at a time and therefore moving the pointer at a faster rate. This is called chunking and is discussed in the next chapter. The purpose of the pointer is to simply guide your eyes as you sweep a page

Left-Sided Pointer

As the name implies, the pointer remains to the side of the left margin at all times. As you read from left to right your eyes use the pointer to mark what line you are on, but not the word. You might this method easier to use because it involves less moving around the page. After you complete reading the line you are on, simply move the pointer down one column and begin from left to right once more.

Subvocalization

Normally, when we read there is a little voice in our head that reads the words back to us. It's a little weird when you think about it. Our inner voice is present at all times yet feels completely natural to us like breathing is. Have you ever tried to breathe manually? The sudden realization that you can control your breath is maddening! (Even if just for a little while before your mind goes to something else and your body takes breaths by itself). Believe it or not, these sounds you hear in your head aren't all metaphysical. There are actual minuscule muscle contractions that take place when you read. The same muscle contractions allow us to speak, but subvocalization contractions can only be detected with specialized equipment.

Subvocalization is thought to play a vital role in the encoding of memory of visual linguistic information to acoustic information. Many people who begin to learn to read (children and adults alike) need corrective subvocalization techniques because they say the words out loud or move their lips and throats as they read. When two readers of different speeds were examined for subvocalization, the faster reader had less brain activation in the areas associated with the visual linguistic encoding than the slower read. This suggests that faster readers achieve these speeds by actively ignoring the need to subvocalize words. Instead, they create a visual cue in their minds coming from the word itself. But this is easier said than done.

Avoiding subvocalization altogether is probably impossible, but there are ways to minimize it from happening. Distraction does wonders to the mind when you are trying to speed read.

Chewing gum, for example, directly interferes with the muscles associated with making subvocalizations in the larynx. As you chew the gum, think about general terms rather than specific words. Focus on the ideas of the passage or sentence rather than what is exactly being said. Another way to distract the mind is by repeating a simple mantra in your head while you read. This is counterintuitive, but it totally works. Instead of subvocalizing the words, your mind will be repeating some pattern, like counting from 1 to 3 over and over again. It does take some practice to master but doing so will emphasize comprehension of ideas over parsing of sentences word by word.

If the mantra doesn't work, you can always try listening to music while speed reading. Choose music that is repetitive, but catchy. I find that music with heavy lyrical content makes it harder to concentrate so I tend to stick with soft electronica or instrumental music when using this technique.

Lastly, if you are using your finger or pencil as a guide, keep your eyes slightly ahead of the position of the pointer. Focus on seeing the words rather than hearing them in your head. Most people will read at the same speed that they talk (thanks, subvocalization!) so if you increase the rate which your eye scans the words, subvocalization will also fall.

Visualization

When you read words, your mind should immediately associate them with images. Instead of hearing the subvocalization ring out in between your ears, draw a mental picture of what the words are saying. This is easier to achieve when you are reading fiction because stories have a natural way of playing out inside your head. If you are a visual learner, you already do this to an extent.

Scanning/Skimming

While not speed reading techniques themselves, scanning and skimming are good practices when getting to know a piece of text. Skimming is the process of quickly moving your eyes over entire passages in a matter of seconds. You aren't really reading because you don't stop to read individual words. Instead, you sort of gloss over them and try to catch big ideas. A few words are going to stand out to you, and from these words, you can gauge what the passage is about. For example, if you skim an article and see the terms "Russian," "Trump," "investigation," "embassy," and "Kremlin," you can easily tell what the passage is getting at. A skilled skimmer can quickly look over an article in a matter of seconds and decide if it is worth their time or not.

Scanning is closely related to skimming, but it is more involved. It still isn't reading though. With scanning, you are looking for specific keywords in the text rather than reading them. You don't really need to scan if you are reading on your computer because most programs allow you to do CTL + F to and they will search the keyword for you.

Keyword Search (Hawk's eye)

This is similar to scanning, but you are actually reading the passage. When you look for keywords you are actively searching the text as you read until you find one that catches your eye. When you do, you slow down and carefully read the sentence to maximize comprehension. You can then create a mental note of the sentence and use it as the main idea of the passage. Once you accumulate enough of these keyword passages you have enough information to start forming relationships between them.

Chapter 8: Comprehension at These Speeds

Okay, now you know some of the basics, and can hopefully perform some semblance of speed reading on your own. It's time to test yourself again, but this time we are concerned with how well you are retaining information. If this is your first time trying to speed read, I can imagine how overwhelming it may feel. Your subvocalization control may be poor, and you still hear the words, but they are sped up, or you only hear every third or fifth word in a sentence. Personally, I still hear the subvocalizations when I do my speed reading, but I can ignore them in most cases. My visualization skills are perform better, and that seems to work well for me. I don't have any word summaries for you, so you will have to do this on your own. Again, pick two passages of low- and high-density writing (different from the previous ones you chose) and read them as fast as you can. Immediately afterward, time yourself 1–3 minutes to recall as much information as you can without looking back at the material. This is just a test to see where you are at with comprehension. Rate yourself on a scale from 1 -7, 1 being no understanding of the text and 7 being a high understanding. If you are anything like me, the low-density material has higher comprehension and it was faster to read than the high-density one.

If you feel like you scored poorly on both, that's fine. What matters here is that you are comfortable with your limits. If you did well on the low-density example, then you can probably read a little faster. The same goes for the high-density example. And if you didn't retain as much information, you can try going slower.

Chunking

Chunking is a technique used to increase reading comprehension. It is also called reading word groups. When you are tracking your reading with your finger or mouse pointer, instead of consciously reading one word at a time try to read several at once. As a beginner, you may want to start at two. That is, move the pointer two words at a time. This takes a little while to practice before it becomes automatic. I can consistently group words in fours, and my reading comprehension remains high at speeds of 600 words per minute. Only small children read one word at a time!

___

Remember those kids in elementary school who took forever to read? I sure do. I didn't go to the best schools, so the pattern of word-by-word reading would persist until my high school years when I took honors classes instead. Reading in chunks both reduces subvocalizations and strengthens your ability to visualize words.

Since I've been using chunking for a while now, I can remember patterns of words that occur frequently, and parse them in a jiffy. Doing this isn't as remarkable as it may sound. It's all just a matter of practice. Mathematician Claude Shannon, famous for creating information theory, once calculated the information entropy of the English language to be 2.62 bits per letter or an average predictability of about 50% (4.5 letters per word on average). Essentially what this means is that English is a 50% redundant language! Yu cn unstnd ths bcse englsh is hgh entropy! In fact, most languages have a degree of redundancy. The same can be said for sentence structure. We all know that most sentences have a noun, a verb, and determiners (the, it, this, etc.). More specifically, every sentence needs a subject and a predicate. Just how your phone has autocorrect, you can "guess" the next word in sequence without having to read it. Clichés are also heavily used in writing. If you see the string of words "Once upon" you can probably guess correctly that the following words will be "a time". There are countless examples of this that you will encounter when speed reading.

Previous Knowledge Association

Remember how memory works by attaching new memories to old ones? The previous knowledge that you accumulate over time allows you to connect novel concepts together, both solidifying your understanding of what you already know and how it relates to new information. When you are speed reading, it helps that you have some familiarity with what is in front of you. I have always been interested in medieval life, especially the type depicted in works of high fantasy. These are usually based off of early European societies. When I was reading Vaclav Smil's book mentioned earlier, many of the early chapters talked about what life was like for the average peasant, what their daily energy intake was (calories) and how they spent their days. Unfortunately, there is no easy way to train previous knowledge association because it is based purely off the things that you know, and the things that interest you the most. The strongest neural connections that exist in your brain will help your speed reading endeavors if you can find a way to link the new information to the old. This all happens very rapidly as you read, to the point that it is automatic like breathing.

Preemptive Vocabulary Building

One of the reasons why reading comprehension goes down the faster you read is that you don't take the time to look up vocabulary. If you don't know what certain words mean then the overall meaning of a sentence can vary drastically from what you parsed it as. It is far too easy to simply "skip" difficult words when you are reading only to later discover that none of what you read made sense. Or worse, if the term is brought up repeatedly throughout the rest of the passage you will be doubly lost. To remedy this, you can try what I call preemptive vocabulary building, which is just a fancy way of saying look up the words before you read. Having a larger vocabulary will aid you both in your reading and writing pursuits and strengthen your memory-keeping a list of vocabulary is a no-brainer! Building vocabulary lists is time-consuming to do for paper books, but easy to do with electronic ones. I have somewhat of a programming background so it is trivial for me to write a program that reads the contents of a .pdf or .epub file and read word frequencies.

If I keep a database of known words, I can take away the missing set and study those new words. You will be amazed at how your reading improves when you don't have to constantly be wracking your brains for a definition that simply isn't there.

You can google around for some online tools that will help you do just this. Some of them allow you to copy and paste passages to get word frequencies or upload a .pdf file. What you can do is keep a database or simply a list of vocabulary words that you have compiled over time. It beats keeping them all in your head, and it makes it easier to compare against the word frequencies of new reading material.

Regression

Regression happens when you go back in the text to reread a sentence or passage because it didn't stick the first time. If you find yourself doing this too often it's a tell-tale sign that you aren't comprehending what you are reading. It is a good speed reading habit to avoid this at all costs. Read the passage once and do not go back. Even if you didn't completely understand what was said, you can use context clues from the following sentences to fill in the blanks. If you keep practicing speed reading, you will find yourself going back less and less. Regressions slow down your overall speed and ultimately are not worth it. Just think, what are the chances that you missed some crucial piece of information and you will regain it after re-reading the same sentence or paragraph? The chances of that happening are pretty slim. A book will give you various context clues along the way. These include chapter titles, subtitles, bullet points, and images. If you are keeping up with your keyword searches, you are less likely to regress when reading random passages. Remember that the English language is redundant, which means all writing to an extent is also redundant. You don't need to understand 100% of what you read to derive value from it.

Exercises for part 2

1. To get familiar with speed reading, pick a book off your shelf (or hard drive) that is easy to digest and is some 300 or so pages long. This will be your practicing book. What I want you to do is speed read as fast as you can and every five pages write a summary of the main points you have read. Time yourself on how long it takes to read five pages (if you can get an exact word

count on an electronic version the better). Say you read five pages in 5 minutes. That's one page a minute, which isn't too bad. Keep doing this exercise and writing the summaries until you finish the book. After each chapter, read over your notes and re-read the chapter at a normal pace and see if your comprehension was correct. The more you practice this the better you will get at understanding what you read

2. Get any reading material and try to chunk your visual understanding by 2 words, then 3 words and so on. Try to master it up to 3 or 4. You don't really need to keep track of this, just do it when you have time. Eventually, you will be chunking by 3, 4 or even more words simply from doing exercise 1.

Part 3:

Write Faster, Write Smarter:

How to go from 2,000 words a day to

10,000

Chapter 9: Understanding Writer's Block and How to Overcome It

Writing has always been a natural interest to me. Growing up, it was my strongest subject at school year after school year. In college, I took classes in creative and technical writing. I was dabbling with writing stories since middle school. I used to create characters in my head for fun and put them on paper when I became bored. There have always been times when I wanted to write something but found that I couldn't. I could stare at a blank piece of paper or word document until my eyes bled and have nothing to show for it. As a consequence, I was always a slow writer. The average 3–4-page essay in school took me hours to finish. The hardest part was getting started. I would write the introductory paragraph and then erase it over and over again because I felt it sounded wrong. I would later learn that doing this is a form perfectionism, and perfectionism has no place in the superhuman's toolbox. A superhuman writes with purpose and has the courage to commit to the words they first put down. This doesn't mean that their work is perfect. It simply means that their work gets finished, published and sold.

Somewhere down the line, you decide whether you want to be that "perfectionist" writer or the prolific one. If you choose the prolific route, you must learn how to write more than just a few thousand words a day. In his memoir *On Writing,* Stephen King recommends that a writer spend no more than 2 -- 3 months working on a novel. This assumes writing for at least four hours a day, for a total of two to three thousand words a day. If you do the math, that equals less than one thousand words a day. Now, I know that Stephen King has published dozens of titles and over a hundred short stories. That doesn't mean that he is a *fast* writer. But ask George R.R. Martin, who is a famously slow writer if he wishes he could write as fast as King. In a recent dialogue between the two, King admitted that he pounds out six pages a day, without fail. When George R. R. Martin asked him if he ever has days when he can't even write a sentence, King responded by saying no, he usually gets the six pages down. That is unless something bad happens as the sayings go.

Six pages a day is astonishing, though I would argue that Stephen King still isn't that fast of a writer. There are countless other authors that output much more books a year than he does. Unquestionably Stephen King's novels are of high quality, so it could be that he has found his personal "sweet spot" between quality and quantity. I don't think anyone wants to be that writer who cranks out book after book only to receive scathing reviews of their work. I believe that every writer has their own sweet spot between quantity and quality. And that it takes a while to reach it. I also believe that a writer who wants to learn how to write faster can also work hard to increase their speed. If you, like R.R. Martin, have difficulties writing at times, it probably comes down to perfectionism or some other defect in the writing process. Martin has a lot to live up to. As of writing, he's still working on the highly anticipated *Winds of Winter* of his Game of Thrones series. A title that has been years in the making now.

Most writers new and old do not have that kind anticipation to live up to. There is no reason to stall for years on a first novel simply because you want to get everything perfect. I believe a novel can be written in well under a month, working a modest four hours a day. Of course, you could speed up completion time by adding more hours. The final chapter in this book includes a method for finishing a novel in less than ten days, but that assumes at least four hours of good work a day.

If you want to write more words a day than you are currently, you need to learn how to overcome writer's block. Despite what you may have been told, writer's block is not inherent to the writing process at all. Those who suffer from it do so because they intend their writing to be the best quality possible. I think this is a mental trap at the root of all instances of writer's block. Writers are full of ideas. And if they aren't, they shouldn't be writing until those ideas are actively flowing in the mind.

As someone who considers themselves a writer, dealing with writer's block has been a lifelong pursuit. I've tried countless ways to get rid of it. A teacher in high school introduced me to "stream of consciousness" writing where you write literally anything that pops into your mind as you write, and you don't stop until you can't go anymore. Even when I tried doing some of those exercises, I would still freeze up and not know what to write next. Saying that I was a timid writer is an understatement. Little by little I learned how to keep writing for longer. I would time myself and do at least one stream of conscious exercise a day. I could write up to 1,000 words in twenty minutes, which is a little above the average typing speed of 40 words a minute. Other times when I couldn't write I simply walked away, went for a stroll or cleaned some portion of my room to get out of my head. This is the same type of diffuse thinking explained in Chapter 5 where you let your mind wander rather than focus on a single thing. Other times I simply sloughed through my writing painfully slow, because I knew that even writing a little bit at a time would be faster than waiting for my mind to think of something.

Origins of Writer's Block

I believe writer's block arises from two primary mechanisms. First is perfectionism, which I already talked about at the beginning of the chapter. The other is due to a lack of direction. If you sit down in front of a computer or paper without knowing what you are going to write about, then you are setting up for failure. A quick little exercise you can do to test your writing direction skills is to imagine a single word or feeling in your head and do a stream of consciousness with that word in mind. Time yourself for 20 minutes and see how many words you can pound out in that time frame. Don't know what word to focus on? Here are some that might help

Dark	Anger	River	Solstice	Ambiguity	Red	Destruction	Elation	Loss	Evasion
System	Conflict	Forest	Puppy	War	Violence	Lust	Earth	Lust	Love

When you have a strong idea or emotion in your head the words just flow out. You don't have to think about a story or plot details because it is a stream of consciousness — you simply write about what your mind associates with that word.

It can very well lead to a narrative or story of sorts, or it can be a total jumble of words and concepts. If you want to become a prolific writer and write up to 10,000 words a day, you need to write somewhere between a stream of consciousness pace and your normal writing one. When you think of a single word it is easy to come up with the next line in a sentence because it is simple. You should strive to be as simple in your normal writing as well. Simple here doesn't mean mechanical sentences and sixth-grade vocabulary, it means simple in purpose and execution. You can still write wonderful and complex sentences when they come from simple ideas. Instead, I would argue that simplifying your ideas allows you to write with more complexity. When your mind isn't cluttered with random thoughts each trying to drown out the other, your speed goes off the charts.

Perfectionism and lack of direction result in the inability to get started on your work. Let's distill these two notions a little bit more. What is perfectionism? The obvious answer doesn't tell us much—it's the desire to make your work stand out the most so that it is flawless. You want your work to be something that you are proud of. Maybe you think back to high school literature class and the classics you studied. I know I sure did when starting out. I wanted to write eloquently like them. To use symbolism and create complex thematic motifs. However, few of us will be able to write with the same eloquence. They are called the "masters" of literature for a reason. Today, few writers can match the same level of mastery as them, and these tend to be hardcore academics. Think of writers like David Foster Wallace. I won't discourage anyone trying to do this type of work, but you probably couldn't produce a classic in one month, let alone a lifetime. The perfectionism definition only tells us the what, and not the why or how. These two can be explained chiefly with one word: fear. Perfectionism is the fear of sounding uneducated or being labeled a bad writer. It is also the fear of failing your own expectations. And if you expect to become the next Kafka, you are setting those expectations high. Imagine working on your novel thinking it will be discussed for decades to come. You wouldn't even know where to start! Dispelling fear begins by lowering your expectations, or what I call "honing your focus". You need to refine the ideas you have about how your writing ought to sound. Heck, even the best-selling works of fiction today are written with simple language. Why? Because they are more digestible by larger audiences. If making money from writing novels is your goal, you needn't have too high expectations for your writing. There is no easy way to overcoming fear other than by simply saying "get over it". As soon as you start writing you are building forward momentum to drive things to completion. As soon as you second guess yourself the momentum is lost. I invite you to write with courage. To never second guess your work until after the drafting stage. See, the more you write the better you will get at it anyway. If you are stuck on square one and you keep revising things, you go into the negatives! Conversely, if you are stuck on square one and you don't move forward, you don't have any momentum to keep going.

Creating the Sense of Direction

The second constituent of writer's block is no obvious sense of direction. You have no idea who the characters are, what the setting is, or even how the plot moves forward. Over the years I've studied the existence of two archetypes of writers. The first type called the plotters like to organize their books from beginning to end. They set up storyboard for their characters and set up outlines for the plot. These types of writers know what they are going to write before they even start. I call the second archetype the write-as-you-gos. Write-as-you-go writers have a vague idea of what to write, and so are more likely to fall into the clutches of writer's block. I've heard every possible argument coming from both schools of

---

thought. The plotters take extra time to devise intricate plotlines and the write-as-you-go writers create an engaging story as they feel it unravel. The problem is that the latter system doesn't work for the majority of people. It sounds tempting to write this way because it's fun, but in the end, you have a frustrated writer who quits their novel mid-way through because they run out of creative steam. The plotter is slow and methodical at first when they are writing the outline, but as soon as they get started, they are off the rails. Not only do they have a clear sense of where the story is taking them, but they also have the creative freedom to change things as they go. After all, outlines CAN be erased and rewritten. Therefore, the plotter gets the best of both approaches. They have direction, and they have the ability to alter the story as they see fit. Although I'm referring to writing a novel here, the principles are the same for any type of writing. Whether that be a non-fiction book, article or even blog post.

If you are a write-as-you-goer, I'm not surprised that you are reading this book. I invite you to take some time to create a simple storyboard or outline, and at the very least write character notes for each of your major characters. After the worldbuilding process is at a solid base, the rest of the story tends to unfold on its own.

The Role of Procrastination and Distractedness

Writer's block goes hand in hand with procrastination. In a way, writer's block *is* procrastinating because you are dreading the act of writing words down only to erase them immediately after because you think they suck. So, the effect is two-fold: you don't know what to write, and you don't want to write what you do end up writing. It sounds tricky, but if you've ever dealt with extreme writer's block then you know what I am talking about. Every time you sit down and write something it just seems off — and you promptly hit the backspace until you are back at square one. If you don't know what to write, you might take this as a cue to do other things to get your mind off the work. This can quickly devolve to more dopamine hit chasing. Remember the importance of setting up the proper learning environment. The same techniques should be used to set up your writing environment. You want to insulate yourself from the outer world of distractions. Turn your phone off (yes, all the way, not just silent) and don't turn it back on until you have written a good chunk.

Instead of reaching for something that will only waste your time, there are some healthier options. Try to free-write as a warm-up exercise if you find yourself in a rut. For me, the free write is a vital part of any writing session. I take 10 to 20 minutes to just write about the things that are going on in my life. Other times I get creative and think of a small little narrative unrelated to the work at hand. Sometimes I do stream of consciousness, but other times I don't. Stream of consciousness helps me get into the habit of putting words down while a more nuanced approach gets my creative juices flowing. Another thing that you can do is to read some material that is related to your work. If you are doing fiction, pick up the latest novel you are reading and knock out a few pages to get the brain going. If you are doing technical work, there are plenty of examples of documentation online. Really, the best activity you can do is making an outline, which you will learn the specifics of how I write them in Chapter 13. Take time to gather up all the background knowledge that your work requires. If you are writing a shootout scene for a crime thriller, maybe look up some facts about the guns that are being fired. What caliber are they, and what type of ammunition is being used? If you go the research route be extra careful not to stray off task. I tend to look up a lot of things on YouTube. As a precaution, I do all my YouTube research in a private browser window so that none of my recommended videos show up in the sidebar.

Otherwise, I would be tempted to watch them.

If you are stuck starting at the beginning or a certain point, there is no rule that says you can't skip around. As you formulate the plot of your novel, for example, you probably think of certain scenes that just have to be in it. If you have any "It would be really cool if this character did x" type of thoughts in your head then go ahead and work on that scene! You will be energized from working on something that excites you, and you may have a better idea of how to write the scene than to do whatever it was you were stuck on.

Chapter 10: How to Write Smarter, Write Faster

The previous chapter was more about fiction writing, but the same principles can be applied to the writer's block experienced by technical and non-fiction writers as well. Writing is just putting down words that are in your head onto paper or the word processor. If you want to write smarter and faster, you must do two things. One, you must learn to write courageously. And two, you must learn to write directedly. Writing courageously only comes with practice. Imagine that you are a noble warrior or marksman and your weapon of choice is the pen (or keyboard). The art of courageous writing, like the art of fighting, takes ardent mental conditioning. But it's not all just pounding at the keys hoping that things get better. It is a craft that you will learn to execute with grace just as any warrior or marksman learns how to use their weapon with grace. You can learn to write directedly by using a simple formula discussed later.

You can think of your mind as a writing factory. The many workers are the neurons that fire together to form ideas, and then send neural impulses to your hands to type or scribble. The goal of the factory is to output as many units (words) as possible. The problem of getting a book out then is a problem of manufacturing. Any factory deals with a number of production constraints (otherwise products would be flying off conveyor belts at the speed of light). The most obvious constraints are time, the quantity of supplies, and the number of workers. The main constraints in your writing factory are the speed at which you can think about ideas, how fast you can physically get those ideas down, and the intervals at which you rest. The average person can type at about 40 wpm. Knowledge professionals who deal with keyboards everyday as part of their jobs and daily lives may get up to 70 wpm. Typing professionals like scribes, typists, transcribers and so on can do over 100 wpm. If you do the math, at a speed of 70 wpm you can expect to write a maximum of 4,200 words per hour. That is assuming that you can 1) type at 70 wpm and 2) you can keep that pace or higher when writing (which is a little more complex than simply typing the keys displayed on your screen). The number 4,200 is effectively the upper bound for words typed per hour for your factory. The most I've ever gotten in one hour was 4,800, but I don't really try to go faster than 4,000 because I can feel the quality of the work perceptibly go down.

I think 4,000 or even 3,500 is a good, modest goal. Any writer who claims they can do more in one hour is simply pushing their luck on the quantity over quality gambit. Even writing at 2,000 words an hour is a huge improvement for writers who habitually deal with writer's block. A typist may be able to get insane speeds, but somebody else is literally telling them what they are supposed to write. Furthermore, just because a job requires 80-95 wpm as a prerequisite It doesn't mean that the typist is holding down this speed all throughout the day. Trust me, even at 2,000 words an hour your fingers will begin to feel it. Another alternative is to use dictation software such as Dragon Naturally Speaking to transcribe spoken word into text. Most people can easily talk up to 150 words per minute, making dictation an interesting option for those who are natural chatterboxes. Personally, not my cup of tea. But if you are an extroverted individual who likes to talk and is good at it, it may be your ticket to upping your writing factory capabilities.

Directiveness: The Who, What, When, Where, Why, and How

Say you are given a new writing assignment at work or you decide to start on a new fiction project. You open up your favorite word processor, open a new file and give it a name. Now what? What are the steps that you must take to complete the assignment on time or make sizeable progress on your projects? The first thing you need to identify is the what. This can be as simple as reading documentation requirements supplied by your employer or setting up some arbitrary amount of work that needs to be done on your project. If you decide to start a novel, for example, you could say that you want to get 3,000 words down before finishing that writing session. Always have an end goal in mind. Next, ask yourself what you are going to write. If you have clear requirements, this is easy. Simply pick some of the low hanging fruit and say "I am going to do tasks x, y, and z". If you are writing fiction, you will need to design an outline or storyboard which you will learn more about in Chapter 13. Many office workers can benefit from using templates for filling out reports. If the writing you do tends to be similar across assignments, you can jumpstart on the what by designing a boilerplate template so that all you need to do is fill out the relevant information. Never go into a writing assignment without knowing what you are going to write. That initial sense of indirection is deadly and can lead to writer's block or worse, procrastination. I cannot stress the importance of preparation enough. If your mind is primed up with ideas and direction, the words will simply roll off the tongue straight into your work. It's also possible to use the memory techniques you learned in part one to aid you in preparation. For any major project, I like to ready up my loci with each chapter I plan on writing. The planning stage takes a little longer, but I can easily recall story details when I begin writing.

Know Your Audience – The Who

This goes without saying, but you should streamline your directiveness depending on who you are writing for. Identifying your audience and pandering your work towards them is another important facet of finding direction. A clear understanding of who your audience is, and how you should write for them is a reassuring piece of information for when you get lost. Are you writing a young adult fiction novel or a more general piece of fiction? Young Adult literature follows well-defined tropes and clichés. There's the love interest, the outsider, the coming of age story, the call to action, you name it. These works are generally targeted at ages 12- 18, so you can imagine what type of language you should use. You want to go for easily digestible chapters and lots and lots of dialogue. Things like symbolism and motifs are not given a premium because it's the plot that matters more. Imagery is also kept to a minimum unless it is documenting various action scenes.

Knowing your audience is relevant in the corporate and business worlds as well. Anyone who has studied technical communication knows the importance of writing for an audience. Audience analysis is the process of running a sort of "audit" between your document requirements and the people who will consume your writing. Are they executives, technicians or end users? What type of information do they hope to gain from your writing, and how can you supply it to them? In other words, what kind of language and tools do you need to best transfer information from your writing to their minds? Audience analysis follows its own who, what, where, when, why and how scheme. Where will the audience be reading the documents? Is it set for online publication or is it an internal document? Are they going to read the document at an upcoming conference? Is it a type of document that they will read once, or will they reference it multiple times? Will they read the document on a digital device like a tablet, or is it confined to a binder or user manual? Finally, why are they reading it? Are they undergoing additional training, or are they doing simple information gathering? There will be some overlap between the answers, and you may have more than one audience, but that's okay. What matters is that you have a plethora of audience-related guidelines that shape the direction of your writing.

Whether you are writing fiction or non-fiction, for technical or non-technical audiences, it is worth creating one or several "audience personas" to solidify these guidelines. Say you are writing a crime thriller with heavy adult themes. Your persona is someone above the age of 18, (or mature teenagers) could be male or female and has an interest in thrillers. It's a good start, but still far too general. You can streamline the process by becoming more specific. Maybe your novel is high in espionage tactics or weapon parlance. If so, maybe your audience belongs to law enforcement agencies or military organizations. If there is a heavy emphasis on romance, your audience persona will definitely be female, maybe the spouse of someone who deals with crime.

Know Your Writing Environment – The Where

Remember how you learned to set up the ideal environment for learning in chapter 3? You can use a similar if not exact replica of your learning environment to begin writing. For me, as long as I have some semblance of four walls and a closed door, I can make do. I couldn't really achieve this level of privacy until I moved out of my parents home, so I had to use libraries and other public yet quiet places to do all my work. I know some writers who prefer to put on music to set the mood. If they are writing a mystery, they will go for jazz and noir. If they are doing fantasy, the put on some of those "Epic Fantasy" music playlists you can find on YouTube. But I prefer silence over noise. If I can't get silence, I will try to use music to drown out the noise. It's really up to you to decide. As always, turn your phone off, and disconnect the internet or open a private browsing window. Private browsing is neat because your browser forgets any saved passwords and logs you out from every site. This is a sort of mental block that will make you think twice before mindlessly opening Facebook or Twitter. When you go to these pages, you will be met by a login screen that tells you (metaphorically at least) to go back to your work.

Know Your Deadlines, Know Your Work Schedule – The When

I have always preferred to get work done immediately after waking up. I do a quick warm-up writing exercise and immediately start where I last left off. I do this for one hour or two before really "getting up" to make breakfast, do chores and shower. I like to think that this primes my mind for the work day ahead, which for me lasts anywhere from three to six hours afterward but potentially many more if I am running on a deadline.

Another part of knowing your work schedule is being able to estimate daily word counts. At the beginning, you can probably give yourself a modest 800–1,000 words per hour. I believe this is easy to achieve if you are constantly planning. Without planning, this number won't be consistent at all. After you learn how to increase your speed this number goes up. You will learn more about planning in the next chapter, as well as how to track your daily progress so that estimation is easier. Always have deadlines in mind. If you can correctly estimate your daily word count and stay consistent, you will never miss a deadline again.

Build knowledge before you embark on the writing journey. Knowledge can be anything, from the personal knowledge you have committed to memory to knowledge that is part of active research. Consolidate all your available information into a solid plan of attack for getting the work done. This can come purely from mental resources with the relevant physical or electronic reference material there only if you need it. A more streamlined approach is the outline, which I have briefly talked about in this chapter. If you have notes or supplementary reading material, go over them once again before you write. Writing a book has a clear set of transitions from beginning to middle and middle to end. If these transitions are all planned beforehand, you can go down the list of events and never have to deal with writer's block creeping up on you. If you aren't writing books, it's a little harder to plan. What you can do is look for a sequential pattern of events or figures in your work and see if you can write an outline for those.

Know Your Motivation – The Why

Ask any fiction writer what their motivation behind their stories are and you get amazing answers. Writers write what they write because they care deeply about things. Some of these are politically based or philosophic in nature but they can also be very simple. J.K. Rowling said that the idea for the *Harry Potter* series simply "came to her" one day. C.S. Lewis wrote the *Narnia* books for his granddaughter Lucy. Though these motivations are simple, they are still effective. Everything that you end up writing will come back to motivation one way or another.

Perhaps you think that your motivation is money. Or that you are only doing the work because your boss or client is paying you for it. In those circumstances, the motivation isn't strictly yours, but the motivation of your audience. Why would somebody want to pick up the thing that you are writing in the first place? What information or experiences are they looking for? Even when you get stuck during the writing or planning phase, coming back to the motivation will help you figure out what to do next.

Developing courage as a writer is not an overnight process. No matter what books or blog posts you read, you won't develop this skill without active practice. The tools at your disposal are writing exercises like stream of consciousness and free writes. Remember the theory of constraints. If you currently type below 70 wpm, learning how to touch type at these speeds will be beneficial to you. I wouldn't worry about learning how to type faster than that, though. The next tool at your disposal which I am about to introduce is the idea of gradual increments of fast typing. You can probably remember times you wrote extremely fast in a state of total concentration or flow, only to taper off back to normal writing speeds or into the clutches of writer's block. Writing stamina is the ability to keep writing at the same pace for extended periods. Think in terms of hours rather than minutes. If you practice writing as quickly as possible in short increments, you can eventually build up endurance.

Depending on how busy you are, aim to complete dozens of these exercises a day. They only take five minutes at a time, but the word count will add up over time. The theory is simple: pick any writing project you are currently working on and go at it wherever you left off in the draft for just five or ten minutes at a time. What's important is that you write and don't ever stop writing until the timer goes off. Forget about spelling and punctuation errors. Just like with speed reading, eliminate backtracking from your process. Say that you complete twelve 5-minute sessions at a speed of 70 wpm every day. That's already 4,200 words! When I first started getting serious about writing fiction, I could barely type at 1,000 words per hour.

Realistically, you are going to struggle to just hit 5 minutes of sustained high-speed writing. At least you will at first. Over time, however, you should begin to see progress. Do as many of these exercises as you can. Start off with maybe 3 or 5 and slowly make your way up. If you find that increasing volume is easy, try to increase duration next. Try for 10 minutes, then 15, then 20, until you get to the hour mark. The beauty of this system is that you can easily integrate with the Pomodoro technique you learned in Chapter 5. Feel free to experiment with your rest periods and the number of Pomodoros you complete in a row.

Finding Balance – Putting It All Together

You write smarter by gathering up all the knowledge related to your work. Either putting it into your mind using the memory techniques learned earlier, or on paper in the form of outlines. Next, you set up your defenses by going down the list of writing directiveness. Your audience personas will allow you to relate to your work on a deeper basis. For extra points, you can pretend that you are the persona and critique your own work as you go. Setting up the correct environment will help you hone your concentration and avoid procrastinating until the working day is done. If you know how to estimate the daily outputs of your writing factory, you know how to gauge your deadlines. When all else is lost, remember your motivation for writing in the first place and find the strength to continue.

You write with courage by overcoming your personal self-doubts. These are the fear of failure and sounding boring or dumb. Ultimately, these fears will put a cap on the number of words you can write a day. The only way to overcome a fear is to face is directly, and you do this through daily accelerated writing exercises that you gradually increase in duration and volume.

Chapter 11: Preparing for Success Outlining, Drafting, and Tracking

No matter how you look at it, your ability to write at a fast pace consistently is determined by how far you can look into the future. If your ideas are all written down somewhere and you have a clearly defined beginning, middle, and end, then you can already see everything that you need to see. The next steps are to simply expand on what you have written in your planning phase. I'm not going to tell you that writing 10k words a day is possible if you simply practice writing every day. No, this level of performance is dependent on your ability to plan for success. The good news is that it is relatively easy

This chapter deals primarily with the writing of fiction and non-fiction works that follow the length of a book. Outlining is possible for other writing tasks, but perhaps in a different format. Since a book is made up of chapters it is simply a matter of writing down the contents for each chapter and then expanding them when you write the draft. There are a few different ways you can do   this, I'll provide examples for each.

Thin Outline

This outline is a more traditional one that follows the top-down, bullet-point list approach. You can expand on each bullet point however you wish when it comes to drafting. Sometimes I start off with this sort of outline then give it some more flesh in a proper paragraph format (which is the next type of outline) but this step may seem unnecessary to you. I'm going to whip a few chapters from a sample plot for the outline to follow.

Title: A Dance of Swords

1. Chapter 1: Into the Unknown
   a. Introduction of the protagonist, a poor peasant boy named Joseph about the age of 16
   b. Introduction to the setting. Alternative fantasy universe called Sombia. Medieval times. Joseph inhabits the island country of Two Mounts. Lives on the family farm that is situated in the mountainous countryside.
   c. Joseph wanted to be a scribe, but due to financial issues is kicked out of school

d. The story begins one night on the farmhouse, when he is awakened by the sounds of cattle being scared
  i. He hops out of his straw bed and grabs a sturdy stick to scare off what he presumes to be wild wolves attacking the cows
  ii. He doesn't find any wolves, only a trail of blood that leads to the woods.
  iii. For whatever reason, he decides he should follow the trail
e. Joseph ends up listening on a goblin camp.
  i. Terrifying noises of goblins celebrating a fresh kill
  ii. Consumption of blood and searing of beef on an open fire (goblins cook their food who knew)
  iii. Joseph stays hidden but he can hear their demonic voices and see their shadows against the treeline
  iv. Goblins had never been spotted on Two Mounts before. What is going on?
f. The next day Joseph tells his Father what happened. Against the wishes of his mother, both set out to check out the camp in broad daylight

  i. Armed with a pitchfork, and father has a sharpened ax

  ii. They find cow remains at the camp, but no goblins

  iii. The stench of goblin leads them to a strange open hole in the ground. Neither father nor son has ever seen something like it in Two Mount

  iv. Obviously a Goblin cave of sorts.

  v. They hear tremors underfoot like the sound of parading goblins running at full speed. The fear they have been discovered, so they run away.

  vi. The cave is found hours from the farmhouse. On the way back, they pick up an artifact of what appears to be goblin jewelry

2. Chapter 2: The Conversation at the inn

  a. Father has a conversation with Joseph telling him not to go into the woods alone. Salvages what is left of their cattle and puts them in a different enclosure

  b. Joseph wants to fight the goblins but his father gives a firm warning. Goblins have never appeared in Two Mounts before.

c. Father goes to town, instructing his only son Joseph to look after the farm, Joseph disobeys and goes into town without his father's knowledge

    i. Something feels different. As sunset approaches, there are fewer people out in the streets. Street vendors have packed early. No youths can be found playing in the streets.

        1. Virtually no sign of the coming Autumn festival

        2. No decorations or festival tents have been propped up.

    ii. Joseph catches up with a friend he knew from school who is now a militia recruit.

        1. Name: Dormsy. A few years older than Joseph but in the same academic class.

        2. Has a thing for sarcasm

    iii. "Goblins have been spotted as far into the town square"

        1. Joseph gathers that militia is preparing for a frontal assault any minute

        2. There is currently a meeting taking place in the town hall to discuss

what to do with goblins. Security is tight only high officials and select notary publics are allowed in

iv. Joseph and Dormsy stroll through the town observing the different safety precautions that people have taken up.

1. Boarded windows
2. Barricaded doors
3. Splattering of Holy Water
   a. Monotheistic religion, but doesn't play a strong role in anything
   b. Country leaders are usually more revered than God
4. "Is this really necessary?" says Joseph
   a. The king believes that the goblins are preparing a massive attack
   b. King is already barricaded in his castle, rumored not to be present at town meeting
   c. Reaffirm that goblins (evil, supernatural creatures) have never been spotted in Two Mounts

5. Joseph is quite about his own encounters with the goblins and says nothing about the hole

v. Both friends come across the inn, which is one of the few structures still lit. From the looks of things (and the smell of food), there is a full house.

   1. Everyone not allowed to go into town hall meeting have congregated here

   2. Joseph and Dormsy listen outside one of the windows

      a. Why do they do this?

      b. There has been a curfew for anyone under 21 not to be out in the streets

         i. Paternalistic society

      c. Joseph can recognize his father's booming voice

         i. "Goblins have attacked my farm!"

         ii. "Why does the king insist on calling on the militia for protection of the town when folks who live in the country have nothing to protect themselves with"

  iii. A few men offer to patrol the general area

 d. Older gentleman speaks up when most of the talk has simmered down

  i. "Has anyone yet wondered why goblins have appeared all of a sudden?"

  ii. "it is as if some portal to hell has been opened"

  iii. "Our country is in no way a threat to those on the mainland"

  iv. Either the goblins are global phenomena or they were somehow summoned on the island

vi. Both friends are caught by a patrol. Joseph goes with his dad and Dorsmy to the barracks

Fleshed Outline

The fleshed outline is written in narrative form rather than as a list of plot elements. It goes very well with the thin outline, but you can start with either one. I will use the same example as before. The fleshed-out outline tends to be shorter, and less informationally dense. You can add additional details, but don't include any plot elements if you are fleshing it out after a thin outline.

Title: A Dance of Swords

Chapter One: Into the Unknown

Joseph Salisbury awoke one night to the sounds of shrieking cattle. The sounds were of imminent danger, and he'd never heard the cows make those noises before. He took only a sturdy stick with him for protection, expecting some starving wolf to have ventured into the farm. He was not trained in combat, coming from a school of scribes but he knew he had to protect the animals. Wolves are skittish anyways and would run at the sight of him. They liked to keep to the woods. It was unusual for them to come this far into the open country. But when he got there, Joseph found no trace of wolves, only a few straggler cows and a trail of blood leading to the woods. Something had broken through the fence line with vigorous force. Was it a thief? The trail led him to a clearing in the forest where he heard terrifying screams. Upon closer inspection, he sees the hideous figures of goblins rising against the shadows. He watches in horror as the creatures dismember the remains of his father's cattle and drink from the blood. The stench of blood and goblin is so overwhelming he almost gags. If he had to guess, there were at least a dozen of them howling with their devilish cries.

In the morning Joseph relents what happened to his father. To his astonishment, Joseph learns that goblins have never been spotted on the island country of Two Mounts. His dad doesn't believe him until Joseph leads him to the campsite. The forest is rife with destruction. There are overturned trees and bones scattered across the clearing. Not too far off they find a strange opening in the ground. As if the earth suddenly gave way to a gaping mouth. A weird melody seems to ooze out like a large creature breathing. They hear tremors from below and both are filled with images of an army of goblins running amok towards the surface. They flee, expecting to see goblin warriors jump out of the hole. However, nothing gives chase and they slow down to catch their breath. In the mad dash, Joseph stumbled over a necklace made out of brittle bones, which he pocketed without telling his father.

Chapter 2: The Conversation at the Inn

Joseph has a conversation with his father and he is told not to ever venture into the woods again by himself. His father tells him that he is heading to the town to see if there is any news, but to stay and look after what remains of the cattle, who were now put in a smaller pen. He mutters that goblins have never been reported on Two Mounts before leaving. Joseph waits a little bit and decides to go to the town as well. He tells nobody of this. His mother doesn't feel well and heads off to bed before sundown. After wisher her a recovery Joseph ventures into town on foot.

In the town, Joseph is shocked to see how quickly the news of goblins has spread. The streets are virtually empty. Its festival season, yet none of the usual stands are set up. There are no children playing outside. Windows are boarded up and doors barricaded from the inside. He sees a pastor going around spilling holy water on the thresholds of people's houses. Next, he spots a friend from the academy named Dormsly who wound up enlisting for the militia. Dormsly tells him all that he knows about the situation. Goblins were spotted far into the town and the King called for a curfew to those who are underage. The militia has also been mobilized. Joseph also learns about the meeting being held in the town hall. Apparently, the militia is expecting a full-blown goblin attack any moment now and important heads are discussing their options. The two friends stroll around the town for a bit, dodging the dirty looks of adults who tell them to go back home. They notice the lights on the Inn are at full blast and can hear a clamor of voices coming from inside. It seems that the townsfolk are having a meeting of their own. Among the voices, Joseph recognizes the booming drawl of his father, who is retelling the story of goblins attacking his cattle, but he does not mention the goblin camp nor the hole that was found some distance from the farmhouse. When all is quiet, a town elder begins to speak about evil forces having been summoned into the country by a belligerent nation. But his ideas are quickly shot down, as Two Mounts has little enemies and is not particularly prosperous compared to others. The Inn becomes quiet again, only to be disrupted by a scuffle coming from outside. The two youths are discovered by a militia patrol. Dormsly is escorted back to the barracks and Joseph returns to the journey home with his father.

The Draft

After your outline is written, take the same information and start writing the actual narrative. I like to chunk the major points from the thin outline so that they correspond to 100 – 300-word intervals but you can organize them however you want. Remember that you are writing with speed but don't let that be an excuse to let your quality go down. The trick is to find a good middle ground that you are comfortable using. Also, aim for the draft to be as close as final as possible. The process of editing will count towards the time it takes to complete a book, so you want to avoid additional drafting. In the past, I would finish a draft only to end up rewriting it. Sometimes I would end up with two or three drafts!

Your outline is law of the land. Whenever you see that your writing slows to a crawl, return to the outline to see where you are at. All major plot events should be set in stone. If you think of something new as you are writing, go ahead and add it but you should resist any major changes or you will be dealing with rewrites.

Tracking Your Progress

This is where your writing speeds increase over time. Recall the five-minute speed writing exercises from before. You are going to want to keep track of every word you write, so you can calculate your words per hour and words per day metrics. You are going to start off with small sessions of 3 to 5 minutes and steadily increase them. The easiest way to do this is using a spreadsheet program like MS Excel, Google Sheets, or LibreOffice Calc. The columns you will need are date, time for writing down the time stamp of when you starting the writing exercise, duration for the number of minutes spent continuously writing, words for the number of words you achieved in that spurt, words per hour to calculate how fast you were typing and finally words per day. Here is an example of what this may look like. Note that the words per day column is simply adding all the words that you wrote for that day.

Date	Time	Duration	Words	Wph	Wpd
11/05/2018	9:30 AM	5:00	180	2,160	804
11/05/2018	10:10 AM	5:00	200	2,400	804
11/05/2018	12:30 PM	5:00	154	1,848	804
11/05/2018	1:45 PM	5:00	120	1,440	804
11/05/2018	3:21 PM	5:00	150	1,800	804

As you increase your word per session count (as well as duration) your words per day will begin to climb. Notice how in this example the writer only spends 25 minutes out of their day to write and still managed to get 804 words in a day. Ask George R.R. Martin how much he would like to write that in a day. And it only took 25 minutes! Imagine how much more progress the writer could do by having more frequent sessions or by increasing their length.

Chapter 12: Writing a Novel in Ten Days

Here I will provide a general framework you can use for pumping out a book in as little as ten days. My methods are simple: dedicate one or two days to plan out the outline and then get to writing. You can go back to the outline at any time, but it should be figured out as soon as you start writing. I'm not saying that I recommend everyone to write at this pace, but I want to show you that it certainly is possible to get a decent draft out in under two weeks' time. The faster you can get it done, the faster you can get started on editing and adding finishing touches. This framework assumes an average of 4 hours spent per day working. If you increase this number, your mileage may vary

Day One – Starting the Outline

Say you want to bang out a quick fantasy book like the one I started for you in the previous chapter. The first thing you want to do is set up your word requirements. How long do you want to make it? A novella is anywhere from 15,000 to 30,000 words in my opinion. A proper novel is on the order of 60,000 + words. Let's say that our book is going to be a modest 50,000 words for starters. The first Harry Potter book is about 77,000 words, and I read that in like three days as a kid.

Okay, let's get a plot going. To simplify things, I will continue the outline from before. This isn't going to be an amazing plot or anything, it's just to give you an idea. I'll skip the chapters I already covered. I won't flesh the outline out too much, I'll let you do that in a later exercise. I will leave out a lot of plot details too, it will be your job to fill these out however you wish.

Chapter One: Into the Unknown

Chapter Two: The Conversation at the Inn

Chapter Three The Raid

- A horde of goblins attacks the town as anticipated. The assault is led by two massive goblin generals Uktor and Yitra.
- The raid is a massive success. Several people reported missing or dead, the militia forces were too spread out to effectively stop the horde
- Joseph and his family are spared

Chapter Four: Alliance from the West

- Kings set a beacon to neighboring nations about the attack.
- The country of Isadora brings a few factions of their prized army to help restore order on Two Mounts
- Joseph goes to the docks to help, meets a young Isodroan warrior princess named Rhina
- Isadoran outpost set up near the countryside in connection to docks

Chapter Five:

- An emaciated goblin ventures into the farm alone.
- Joseph engages it with his dad's ax and basic leather armor.
- He takes injuries but is victorious in the end
- Puts the goblin in a sack and heads out for the outpost to hand the goblin over to the Isadorans (and to see Rhina)

Day Two – Finish Outline

When you are working on the outline it is your job to ensure the story has a logical beginning and end. You should take your time to get the details right as well as possible. Use the power of visualization to recreate a movie reel in your head about the story. As you write plot elements, take a mental note of the different scenes that you want to include for each. I won't finish the outline for you. Add as many chapters as you want, but keep word requirements in mind. The more plot elements you include the more words you will need for that chapter

Day Two Onwards – Begin Writing

As soon as the outline is finished, it's time to begin writing. If you give yourself at least four hours of work a day you can calculate how fast you need to be writing. So, we have 66,000 total words, and either 8 or 7 days to complete them depending on when you start writing. This is anywhere from 6,250 words a day to 7,142 words a day. For an hourly word count of 1,562 at the low end and 1,781 at the high end. This is assuming the minimal 4 hours of work a day, which you can go over whenever you like. Here is an example Pomodoro table for a single day

Pomodoro	Word Count
30:00	861

30:00	757
30:00	900
30:00	600
30:00	500
30:00	600
30:00	671
30:00	890

Here are eight Pomodoros of 30 minutes each equaling 4 hours of work. If you add up the word counts you get 5.779 which is still some 500 words off from our goal but look at those numbers! How hard is it to get 800 words done in 30 minutes? If your outline is solid and if you don't add too many changes to the plot, there is no reason why you shouldn't be able to hit these requirements. Finishing the book is just a matter of applying your self-discipline skills to completion. You can even work on the outline on your off-time if you use a cloud application like google docs and a smartphone or tablet. Commit to memory where you are at in your daily writing and adjust the plot as needed.

Exercises for Part 3

1. See how fast you can create directionality for a short story using just three words. Find an online tool (or do it yourself) to generate a random noun, followed by a random verb and another noun. Combine these three words in some way in the story. Write for 20 minutes after a 5 – 10-minute planning period. See how many words per hour you can type

2. Finish the outline for the story I started on Chapter 13. Use Either the thin outline or fleshed outline format

3. Write a novel in ten days. Use the story I started or make up your own

Conclusion

Congratulations! You made it through *Becoming Superhuman*. I truly hope you learned a thing or two, and that you take your time to complete the exercises at the end of each part. I also hope that you like me decide to go on the superhuman journey. It's definitely not for everyone.

You still have so much work to do to though. There are countless more books to read and learn about. You can look up "the art of memory" online to read more about the memory techniques first developed by the Greeks. There is also the concept of Vedic math from the Hindus that consists of techniques for doing blazing fast arithmetic in your head. I use both of these things in my daily life.

Always be reading. Always be striving to increase your speed and your ability to retain information. The world is one huge pitcher of information for you to gorge on. Finally, remember to make it a habit to write. Writing every day with directiveness and purpose will teach you how to get those words per hour to new levels.

Finally, if you found this book useful in any way, a review is always appreciated!

Made in United States
North Haven, CT
19 March 2023